Contents

Contents

Contents

Foreword

Welcome to the new edition of *Cite them right: the essential referencing guide. Cite them right* offers advice on how to develop lifelong academic skills in categorising sources of information and providing evidence to support your arguments. This book will support you from secondary-school assignments through to postgraduate research, in writing reports for employers or writing your own publications.

Since the previous edition of *Cite them right* was published in 2005, the scale of electronic publishing has exceeded all predictions. The Internet has become a medium through which anyone can publish and communicate. It is now more likely that with the exception of books (and even here e-books are making a significant impact), most students will be locating information online. Journal and newspaper articles are available online, as are growing collections of audio-visual material, archival sources, scientific data and legal, business and government publications. New sources of information have appeared since the previous edition, whilst readers requested examples of artistic and genealogical sources; examples have been provided for these.

New referencing criteria have emerged, including Digital Object Identifiers (DOIs), stable URLs and article numbers rather than the traditional volume, issue and page numbers. These developments are not uniformly practised in all subjects, with the sciences employing these new referencing methods more frequently than the humanities. As the world of information moves from print to online predominance both the traditional volume, issue, page numbers and the DOI or article number forms are acceptable. This book provides examples for referencing sources of information in print and online versions where possible. Please note that a few of these examples are fictitious and are used to illustrate as clearly as possible what you need to include in citations and references.

How to use *Cite them right*

Section A provides an overview of what referencing is and how to avoid plagiarism. **Sections B** and **C** introduce the conventions for citing information sources in your writing and in the reference list or bibliography that you are expected to provide at the end of each piece of work. **Section D** is a comprehensive list of sources of information with examples of how to cite these in the text of your work and in a reference list or bibliography. You are not expected to read *Cite them right* from cover to cover. Use the contents and index pages to identify where in the book you will find advice on referencing each type of source.

Most of the examples in *Cite them right* are given in an author-date referencing style commonly known as Harvard style. This style emphasises names of authors and the publication years of their work. There is no single authority to define "Harvard" style, hence there are many versions of Harvard in use. *Cite them right* brings together the most commonly used format for author-date references and the most comprehensive range of sources used by today's students and researchers.

Readers have also asked for examples of referencing styles other than Harvard, so in **Section E** examples are provided for referencing the most commonly used sources (books, articles and web pages) in American Psychological Association, Modern Language Association and Modern Humanities Research Association referencing styles. There is also a guide to using the Oxford Standard for Citing of Legal Authorities (OSCOLA) used by many law schools.

For advice on referencing other sources in these styles, check the examples in the Harvard section for which elements of a reference to include and format these in your preferred referencing style. Once you have established which referencing style to use, **stick to it consistently**.

The authors welcome any comments on improving the functionality of *Cite them right* and suggestions of new sources to include. Thank you for using this guide.

Foreword

Section A. An introduction to referencing and how to avoid plagiarism

What is referencing?

The ability to present your ideas to other people is a key lifelong skill. It calls for time and practice to gather information, assess its relevance to your task, read and form your opinions and then share your contribution, verbally or in writing, with others. Within the process of researching and presenting your own work is another key skill: how to represent what you have learned from earlier authors.

When writing a piece of work, whether essay, seminar paper, dissertation, project or article, it is essential that detailed and precise information on all sources consulted is included in your text and in the reference list at the end of your work. This allows the reader to locate the information used and to check, if necessary, the evidence on which your discussion or argument is based. References should, therefore, enable the user to find the source of documents as quickly and easily as possible. You need to identify these documents by citing them in the text of your assignment (called **citations** or **in-text citations**) and referencing them at the end of your assignment (called the **reference list** or **end-text citations**). The reference list only includes sources cited in the text of your assignment as in-text citations. It is not the same thing as a **bibliography**, which uses the same format or reference system as a reference list, but also includes all material used in the preparation of your work. See the **Glossary** in **Section F** for more information on these terms.

Why should I cite and reference sources?

Besides the reasons given above, there are a number of other important reasons why you should cite and reference your sources. In addition to adding weight to your discussion and arguments, references also show that you have read widely on the subject and considered and analysed the writings of others. Appropriately used, references can strengthen your writing and can help you attain a better mark or grade.

They can also:

- Show your tutor/reader what you have read and allow them to appreciate your contribution to the subject

- Establish the credibility and authority of your ideas and arguments

- Demonstrate that you have spent time in locating, reading and analysing material and formed your own views and opinions

What is plagiarism?

Plagiarism is a specific form of cheating and is generally defined as presenting someone else's work or ideas as your own. These works or ideas may be in printed or electronic format and, in all cases, giving credit to the original authors by citing and referencing your sources is the only way to use other people's work without plagiarising.

All of the following are considered forms of plagiarism:

- Using another person's work or ideas (for example, copying and pasting text or images from the Internet) without crediting (citing) the original source

- Passing off someone else's work as your own

- Failing to put a quotation in quotation marks

- Quoting, summarising or paraphrasing (see **Glossary** in **Section F** for definitions of these terms) material in your work without citing the original source

- Changing words or phrases but copying the sentence structure of a source and not crediting the original author

- Citing sources you did not use.

It is even possible to plagiarise yourself if you paraphrase or copy from work you submitted elsewhere without acknowledging the fact through citation and referencing!

How to avoid plagiarism

The fundamental principle is to acknowledge the work of others by providing citations to your references so that the reader can refer to these and other works if they want. It is also helpful to note the following points:

- Manage your time and plan your work - ensure you have time to prepare, read and write

- Use your own ideas and words

- Use the ideas of others sparingly and only to support or reinforce your own argument

- When taking notes, include complete reference information for each item you use

- When using material on the Internet make a note of the source (author, title, URL etc.) and the date that you accessed the page

- Use quotation marks when directly stating another person's words and include the source in your list of references. Doing none or only one of these is not acceptable

- Avoid using someone else's work with only minor cosmetic changes, e.g. using "strong" for "robust" or changing a sentence around

- When paraphrasing, use words or a sentence structure different from the original work and acknowledge the source through in-text citation immediately following the paraphrase

- Save all your notes, printouts etc. until you receive your final mark or grade for the assignment

- Remember that your list of references (sources you have cited) at the end of your assignment is not the same as a bibliography which also includes items (books, articles, web pages etc.) that you used for your research but did not cite directly. Remember, ultimate responsibility for avoiding plagiarism rests with you!

What about common knowledge?

In all academic or professional fields, experts regard some ideas as "common knowledge". This is generally defined as facts, dates, events and information that are expected to be known by someone studying or working in a particular field. The facts can be found in numerous places and are likely to be known by many people: for example, that Margaret Thatcher was a British Prime Minister. Such information does not generally have to be referenced. However, as a student you may only have just started to study a particular subject so the material you are reading may not yet be "common knowledge" to you. In order to decide if the material you want to use in your

Referencing and avoiding plagiarism

assignment constitutes "common knowledge" you need to ask yourself the following questions:

- Did I know this information before I started my course?

- Did this information/idea come from my own brain?

If the answer to either or both of the questions is "no" then the information is **not** "common knowledge" to you. In these cases you need to cite and reference your source(s).

What about confidential information?

If you wish to use source material that is confidential (for example, some legal or medical information) you must obtain permission from all those who might be affected by its publication. If material is in the public domain you are usually free to reference it but, **if in any doubt, ask whoever produced or published the information for permission to use it**.

Which referencing style should I use?

There are many styles of referencing and this is a cause of understandable confusion for many students and authors who may be asked to use different styles for different pieces of work. There are two principal methods of referencing:

- Author-date referencing styles (such as Harvard and APA) which emphasise the name of the author and publication year in the text and full bibliographic details in a reference list

- Numeric styles (such as MHRA and OSCOLA) which provide a **superscript number** (see **Glossary**) in the text with full bibliographic details in footnotes and bibliographies

You will need to check which style is required for your work. In further and higher education your department or faculty may have decided to use a certain style. Others may follow a referencing style agreed by professional authorities, for example the American Psychological Association (known as APA) or the Oxford Standard for Citation of Legal Authorities (known as OSCOLA) which is used by many Law departments in the United Kingdom. If you are writing for an academic journal or newspaper you will need to establish the preferred style of writing and referencing: this information is often given on the publisher's website or will be available from the editor. **Once you have established the referencing style required, use it consistently throughout your piece of work.**

Despite the many referencing styles used in education and literature, the reasons for referencing your sources and the details that you will need to give your readers remain the same. Your aim will be to give the reader all of the information required to find the sources you have used.

Section B. How should I set out citations and quotations in my text?

In-text citations give the brief (abbreviated) details of the work which you are quoting from, or to which you are referring in your text. These citations will then link to the full reference in your **reference list** and **bibliography** at the end of your work, which is arranged in alphabetical order by author.

Your citations should follow this format:

• Author or editor's surname

• Year of publication, followed by a comma

• Page number(s).

If you are quoting directly from a specific page or pages of a work you must include the page number(s). Insert the abbreviation p. (or pp.) before the page number(s).

If your citation refers to a complete work or to ideas that run through an entire work your citation would simply use the author and date details (see the second example below).

Examples

Harris (2008, p.56) argued that "nursing staff ..."

In a recent study (Evans, 2008), qualifications of school-leavers were analysed ...

Often a tutor or supervisor will advise you

on their preferred format for including citations in your sentences. However, as shown by the examples above and below, there are several ways in which you can put them in your text.

When citing publications by up to three authors or editors, all are listed:

Examples

Recent educational research (Lewis and Jones, 2008) has shown that ...

In a newly-published survey Hill, Smith and Reid (2008, p.93) argue that ...

It has been found that "newly-qualified teachers are more likely to become involved in extra-curricular activities than their longer-serving colleagues" (Hill, Smith and Reid, 2008, p.142).

For publications by more than three authors or editors, cite the first name listed in the work followed by *et al*. (see **Glossary**)

Example

New research on health awareness (Tipton *et al*., 2008, p.124) ...

N.B. All authors'/editors' names would be given in your reference list (no matter how many there are) so that each author or editor can receive credit for their research and published work.

Citing multiple sources

If you need to refer to two or more publications at the same time, these can be listed separated by semicolons (;).

Setting out citations and quotations

The publications should be cited chronologically by year of publication with the most recent source first. If more than one work is published in the same year then they should be listed alphabetically by author/editor.

Example

Recent environmental studies (Williams, 2007; Andrews *et al.*, 2005; Martin and Richards, 2004; Town, 2004) considered ...

Citing multiple-author edited publications

If you want to cite a book edited by Holmes and Baker which has, for example, ten contributors and does not specify who wrote each section or chapter, follow the format of citing using the editors' names.

Example

Recent research (Holmes and Baker 2008, pp.411-428) proved ...

N.B. See **Section D1.6 - Chapters/sections of edited books** for the relevant information on citing and referencing when the author's name is given for a specific chapter or section.

Citing multiple publications published in the same year by the same author(s)

Sometimes you may need to cite two (or more) publications by an author (or authors/editors) published in the same year. You will need to distinguish between multiple items in the text and in the reference list. You do this by allocating lower case letters in alphabetical order after the publication date.

Example

In his study of the work of Rubens, Miller (2006a, p.18) emphasised the painter's mastery of drama in his larger compositions. However, his final analysis on this subject (Miller, 2006b, pp. 143-152) argued that ...

In your reference list, the publications would be shown thus:

Example

Miller, S. (2006a) *The Flemish masters*. London: Phaidon Press.

Miller, S. (2006b) *Rubens and his art*. London: Killington Press.

To cite different editions of the same work by the same author, separate the dates of publication with a semicolon.

Example

In both editions (Hawksworth, 2007; 2002) ...

Where the name of an author/editor cannot by identified, use the title.

Example

In a recent study (*Health of the nation*, 2008, p.94), statistics showed ...

Where the date of a work cannot be identified, use the phrase 'no date' (see example overleaf).

Example

In an interesting survey of youth participation in sport, the authors (Harvey and Williams, no date, pp. 243-245) conclude that much research has concentrated on ...

Where both author and date are unknown, the citation would look like this:

Example

Integrated transport systems clearly work (*Trends in European transport systems*, no date, p. 49).

If you are citing a web page it should follow the guidelines above, citing by: author and date where possible; by title and date if there is no identifiable author or by URL (see **Glossary**) if neither author nor title can be identified.

Example

The latest survey of health professionals (http://www.onlinehealthsurvey.org, 2008) reveals that ...

For more details on how to cite and reference web pages see **Section D8.**

Setting out quotations in your text

Quotations should be relevant to your argument and used judiciously in your text. Excessive use of quotations can disrupt the flow of your writing and prevent the reader from following the logic of your reasoning.

Short quotations, up to two or three lines, can be set in quotation marks (single or double - be consistent) and included in the body of your text.

Example

Bryson (2004, p.156) commented that "If you need to illustrate the idea of nineteenth century America as a land of opportunity, you could hardly improve on the life of Albert Michelson".

Longer quotations should be entered as a separate paragraph and indented from the main text. Quotation marks are not required.

Example

King (1997) describes the intertwining of fate and memory in many evocative passages, such as:

So the three of them rode towards their end of the Great Road, while summer lay all about them, breathless as a gasp. Roland looked up and saw something that made him forget all about the Wizard's Rainbow. It was his mother, leaning out of her apartment's bedroom window: the oval of her face surrounded by the timeless gray stone of the castle's west wing. (King, 1997, pp.553-554).

Paraphrasing

When you paraphrase, you express someone else's writing in your own words, usually to achieve greater clarity. This is an alternative way of referring to an author's ideas or arguments without using direct quotations from their text. Used properly, it has the added benefit of fitting more neatly into your own style of writing and allows you to demonstrate that you really do understand what the author is saying. However, you must ensure that you do not change the original meaning and you must still cite and reference your source of information.

Example

Harrison (2007, p.48) clearly distinguishes between the historical growth of the larger European nation states and the roots of their languages and linguistic development, particularly during the fifteenth and sixteenth centuries. At this time, imperial goals and outward expansion were paramount for many of the countries, and the effects of spending on these activities often led to internal conflict.

Summarising

When you summarise, you provide a brief statement of the main points of an article, web page, chapter or book. This differs from paraphrasing as it only lists the main topics or headings, with most of the detailed information being left out.

Example

Nevertheless, one important study (Harrison, 2007) looks closely at the historical and linguistic links between European races and cultures over the past five hundred years.

Making changes to quotations

If you omit part of the quotation, this is indicated by using three dots … (called ellipsis).

Example

"Drug prevention … efforts backed this up" (Gardner, 2007, p.49).

If you want to insert your own words, or different words, into a quotation, put them in square brackets [ ].

Example

"In this field [crime prevention], community support officers …" (Higgins, 2008, p.17).

If you want to point out an error in a quotation (for example, a spelling mistake) do not correct it; instead write [*sic*].

Example

Williams (2008, p.86) noted that "builders maid [*sic*] bricks".

NB. If you are quoting from historical material, before spellings were standardised, decide to either retain the original spelling, or modernise the spelling and note this in your text.

Examples

"Hast thou not removed one Grain of Dirt and Rhubbish?" (Kent, 1727, p.2).

"Have you not removed one grain of dirt or rubbish?" (Kent, 1727, p.2, spelling modernised).

If you want to emphasise something in a quotation, you can put the emphasised words in italics and state that you have added the emphasis.

Setting out citations and quotations

Example

"Large numbers of *women* are more prepared to support eco-friendly projects" (Denby, 2006, p.78, my italics).

If the original text uses italics, state that the italics are in the original source.

Example

"The dictionary is based on *rigorous analysis* of the grammar of the language" (Soanes, 2004, p.2, italics in original).

Secondary referencing - citing the work of one author when it has been cited in the work of another author

In some cases you will read a source which refers to the work of someone else. This can be shown in your citation by using the phrase "cited in" or other variations, and by giving the page number on which your source cited that information.

Examples

Murray's conclusion (2007, p.82) supports the views of White (2001, cited in Murray, 2007, p. 82) on genetic abnormalities in crops.

There was further evidence to support researchers' views on genetic abnormalities in crops (White, 2001, cited in Murray, 2007, p.82).

Murray (2007, p.82), citing White's views on genetic abnormalities in crops (2001), supports the view that ...

If you have only read Murray's work, then you can only provide full details of Murray's publication in your reference list or bibliography. You cannot include full details of White's work in your reference list unless you have read his/her work yourself and corroborated the facts to which Murray refers. Ideally, you should try to read both Murray's and White's publications so that you can cite and reference both fully.

Section C. How should I set out references in my reference list and bibliography?

What to include in your references

In the Harvard (author-date) system, your references link with your **in-text citations** so that the reader can confirm the full publication details of the work cited in your text and be able to locate it.

Example

In-text citation:

In a recently published survey (Hill, Smith and Reid, 2008, p.93) the authors argue that ...

Reference list:

Hill, P., Smith, R. and Reid, L. (2008) *Education in the 21st century.* London: Educational Research Press.

Works cited in appendices, but not in the main body of your text, should still be included in your reference list/ bibliography.

Authors/Editors

- Put the surname/last name first, followed by the initial(s) of forenames/ first names - for example, Smith, G. R.

- Include **all** contributing names in the order they appear on the title page - for example, Hill, P., Smith, R. and Reid, L.

- Some publications are written/produced by corporate bodies or organisations and you can use this name as the author - for example, University of Cumbria Learning and Information Services. Note that the corporate author may also be the publisher

- If the publication is compiled by an editor or editors, signify this by using the abbreviation (ed.) or (eds.) - for example, Parker, G. and Rouxeville, A. (eds.)

- Do not use "Anon" if the author/editor is anonymous or no author/editor can be identified. Use the title of the work.

Year of publication

- The year of publication (or year when a web page was last updated) is given in round brackets (parentheses) after the author's/editor's name - for example, (2007)

- Other date information (e.g. volume, part number or day and month of publication for journal or newspaper articles, or for forms of personal correspondence) is given after the publication's title - for example, for journal articles: 84(5); or for newspaper articles: 15 August. This information is generally found on the cover or title page of the publication. More detailed examples relating to specific sources are given in **Section D**

- If no date of publication can be identified, use (no date) - for example, Smith, L. (no date).

Title

- Use the title as given on the title page of the book, together with the subtitle (if any) - for example, *Studying and working in Spain: a student guide*

- Capitalise the first letter of the first word of the title and any **proper nouns** (see **Glossary**) - for example, *A history of Shakespearean England*

- In most cases (title of book, journal etc) you would use italics for the publication title - for example, *A brief history of time.*

See further information below regarding journal/newspaper article titles and journal/newspaper titles.

Edition

- Only include the edition number if it is not the first edition

- Edition is abbreviated to edn. (to avoid confusion with the abbreviation ed. or eds. for editor or editors) - for example 3rd edn.

Place of publication and publisher

- These are included (for books) in the order, Place of publication: publisher and are separated by a colon - for example, London: Initial Music Publishing. Usually, you will find the details of place of publication and publisher on the back of the title page.

Page reference

- Usually you do not need to include the number of pages for a book, etc., in the reference list as your in-text citation will either note the exact page(s) of a quotation or simply note the author and date if you are referring to the whole

work. However, if you are referring to a specific chapter/section by the author(s), include the page numbers of the chapter after the publisher's details, for example, London: River Press, pp. 90-99.

Series

- Include series and individual volume number, if relevant, in round brackets after the publisher - for example, Oxford: Clio Press (World Bibliographical Series, 60).

Title of journal/newspaper article

- Use the title given at the beginning of the article

- Capitalise the first letter of the first word of the title and any proper nouns (see **Glossary**)

- Put the title of the article in single quotation marks - for example, 'Britain, Spain and the Gibraltar question'.

Title of journal/newspaper

- Use the title given on the journal/ newspaper front cover

- Capitalise the first letter of each word in the title, except for linking words such as and, of, the, for

- Put the title of the journal/newspaper in italics - for example, *Bulletin of Hispanic Studies, New York Times*

- It is common in the sciences to abbreviate the titles of journals, for example *Journal of Physics D: Applied Physics* is abbreviated to *J. Phys. D: Appl. Phys.* These abbreviations are given on the title page of the article. Check with your assessors if they prefer the abbreviated or full title of journals in your references.

Issue information

- For serial publications (journals, newspapers etc.) you need to include the following information, when given, in the order volume number, followed by issue/part number in round brackets, date or season - for example, 87(3), Summer; or 238(3), 19 July.

URL (Uniform/Universal Resource Locator)

- When referencing a web page you include the same details as you would for a book (author, title, publisher/producer etc.). Similarly, if some details are not available you simply use the next unique element that is provided - for example, if there is no author noted you would reference (and cite) by title - for example, *Trends in tourism* (2008)..

- When referencing web pages or any other Internet documents you must include the full URL as it appears in the **address bar** (see **Glossary**) to avoid any confusion when someone tries to check your reference - for example, http://en.wikipedia.org/wiki/Harvard_ referencing (Accessed: 28 June 2008)

- Include the date you accessed a web page, as in the example above.

Online information using Digital Object Identifiers (DOIs)

Internet pages are identified by a Uniform Resource Locator (URL) but these may change if the owner of the Internet site moves the pages to another host. A system of Digital Object Identifiers is being introduced, which tag individual digital (online) sources. These sources can be anything from journal articles, conference papers and presentations to videos. In the case of a journal article, the DOI includes a number identifying the publisher, the publication, the volume, issue and first page number of an article. This example from the *Astronomical Journal* shows how the DOI replaces the URL in the reference:

Example

Horch, E.P., van Altena, W.F., Cyr, W.M., Kinsman-Smith, L., Srivastava, A. and Zhou, J. (2008) 'Charge-coupled device speckle observations of binary stars with the WIYN telescope. V. Measures during 2001-2006', *Astronomical Journal*, 136, pp. 312-322. DOI: 10.1088/0004-6256/136/1/312 (Accessed: 7 July 2008).

You can locate a source by entering its DOI in an Internet search engine. At present the use of DOIs is more common in the sciences than in other subjects, but the system is likely to expand in future to cover all subjects.

For more information on DOIs see the website of the International Digital Object Identifier Foundation at http://www.doi.org/

Journal articles using article numbers and DOIs

With many journals published on the Internet some publishers, particularly in the sciences, use article numbers instead of issue and page numbers. Each article has a new set of page numbers, rather than the traditional model of a single set of page numbers running through all of the articles in an issue. The reference to the article includes the number of pages in the article. If you are quoting from a specific page in the article, use the page number within the article. The example below uses an article number and a Digital Object Identifier in the reference:

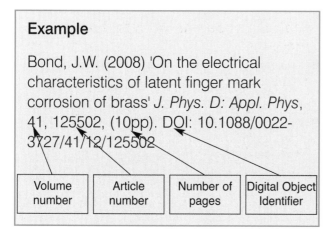

Example

Bond, J.W. (2008) 'On the electrical characteristics of latent finger mark corrosion of brass' *J. Phys. D: Appl. Phys*, 41, 125502, (10pp). DOI: 10.1088/0022-3727/41/12/125502

| Volume number | Article number | Number of pages | Digital Object Identifier |

Unpublished works

You can cite and reference unpublished documents, research etc. just as you do for published works, including all available information. You must make it clear however that the work remains unpublished - for example, Wendell, R. (2007) *Training for primary healthcare*. Unpublished PhD thesis. University of Blaydon.

For examples of how all this information looks in references, see the **sample text** and **reference list** below.

Sample text using Harvard (author-date) referencing style

The latest survey of health professionals (http://www.onlinehealthsurvey.org, 2008) reveals that over 65% are concerned by standards of care for young people in care. This confirms the findings of

Goddard and Barrett (2007) and Franklin (2002). Care workers need additional support (Thomas, 2007, pp.37-46) and Liu *et al.* (2008, p.31-2) have suggested additional measures that could be introduced.

Harvard (author-date) reference list for the above text:

Franklin, A.W. (2002) 'Management of the problem', in Smith, S.M. (ed.) *The maltreatment of children*. Lancaster: MTP, pp. 83-95.

Goddard, J. and Barrett, S. (2007) *The health needs of young people leaving care*. Norwich: School of Social Work and Psychosocial Studies, University of East Anglia.

http://www.onlinehealthsurvey.org (2008).

Liu, B.C., Ivers, R., Norton, R., Boufous, S., Blows, S. and Lo, S.K. (2008) 'Review of professional training', *Cochrane Database of Systematic Reviews*, 2, *Ovid* [Online]. Available at: http://ovidsp.uk.ovid.com/spb/ovidweb.cgi (Accessed: 23 June 2008).

Thomas, R. (2007) *Training for care workers*. Unpublished PhD thesis. University of Blaydon.

Checklist of what to include for most common information sources

	Author	Year of publication	Title of article/ chapter	Title of publication	Issue information	Place of publication	Publisher	Edition	Page number(s)	URL	Date accessed
Book	✓	✓		✓		✓	✓	✓			
Chapter from book	✓	✓	✓	✓		✓	✓	✓	✓		
Journal article	✓	✓	✓	✓	✓				✓		
Electronic journal article	✓	✓	✓	✓	✓				✓	✓	✓
Internet site	✓	✓		✓						✓	✓
Newspaper article	✓	✓	✓	✓	✓				✓		

Setting out references

Section D. How to cite and reference sources using the Harvard (author-date) style

NB Before looking at specific examples in this section you should ensure that you have read about the basics of content and layout in **Sections B** and **C**.

1. Books

1.1 Information in books

Citation order:

- Author/editor
- Year of publication (in round brackets)
- Title (in italics)
- Edition (only include the edition number if it is not the first edition)
- Place of publication: Publisher
- Series and volume number (where relevant)

Example: book with one author

In-text citation:

According to Bell (2005, p.23) the most important part of the research process is …

Reference list:

Bell, J. (2005) *Doing your research project*. 4th edn. Maidenhead: Open University Press.

Example: book with two or three authors

In-text citation:

Goddard and Barrett (2007) suggested …

Reference list:

Goddard, J. and Barrett, S. (2007) *The health needs of young people leaving care*. Norwich: University of East Anglia, School of Social Work and Psychosocial Studies.

Example: book with more than three authors

In-text citation:

This was proved by Young *et al.* (2005) …

Reference list:

Young, H.D., Freedman, R.A., Sandin, T. and Ford, A. (2000) *Sears and Zemansky's university physics*. 10th edn. San Francisco: Addison-Wesley.

Example: book with an editor

In-text citation:

The formation of professions was examined in Prest (1987).

Reference list:

Prest, W. (ed.) (1987) *The professions in early modern England*. London: Croom Helm.

Example: book with no author

In-text citation:

The Percy tomb has been described as "one of the master-pieces of medieval European art" (*Treasures of Britain*, 1990, p.84).

Reference list:

Treasures of Britain and treasures of Ireland (1990) London: Reader's Digest Association Ltd.

1.2 Electronic books (e-books)

Citation order:

* Author
* Year of publication of book (in round brackets)
* Title of book (in italics)
* Name of e-book collection (in italics)
* [Online]
* Available at: URL
* (Accessed: date)

Example

In-text citation:

In their analysis Graham and Marvin (2001, pp.36-92) …

Reference list:

Graham, S. and Marvin, S. (2001) *Splintering urbanism: networked infrastructures, technological mobilities and the urban condition. NetLibrary* [Online]. Available at: http://www.netlibrary.com (Accessed: 23 June 2008).

1.3 Historical books in online collections

Citation order:

* Author
* Year of publication (in round brackets)
* Title of publication (in italics)
* Title of online collection (in italics)
* [Online]
* Available at: URL
* (Accessed: date)

Example

In-text citation:

Adam's measured plans, (Adam, 1764) …

Reference list:

Adam, R. (1764) *Ruins of the palace of the Emperor Diocletian at Spalatro in Dalmatia. Eighteenth Century Collections Online* [Online]. Available at: http://galenet.galegroup.com/servlet/ECCO (Accessed: 2 June 2008).

Example

In-text citation:

An early contribution by Henry (1823) …

Reference list:

Henry, W. (1823) *The elements of experimental chemistry. Google Books* [Online]. Available at: http://books.google.com/books?id=shcAAAAAQAAJ&dq=chemistry&lr=&as_brr=1 (Accessed: 2 June 2008).

1.4 Reprint editions

For reprints of old books, usually only the year of the original publication (not the publisher) is given along with the full publication facts of the reprint.

Example

In-text citation:

One of the first critics of obfuscation (David, 1968) ...

Reference list:

David, M. (1968) *Towards honesty in public relations*. Reprint, London: B.Y. Jove, 1990.

1.5 Translated books

Example

In-text citation:

In his biography of Bach, Schweitzer (1911, p.32) considered ...

Reference list:

Schweitzer, A. (1911) *J.S. Bach*. Translated by Ernest Newman. Reprint, New York: Dover Publications, 1966.

1.6 Chapters/sections of edited books

Citation order:

- Author of the chapter/section (surname followed by initials)
- Year of publication (in round brackets)
- Title of chapter/section (in single quotation marks)
- 'in' plus author/editor of book
- Title of book (in italics)

- Place of publication: Publisher
- Page reference

Example

In-text citation:

The view proposed by Franklin (2002, p.88) ...

Reference list:

Franklin, A.W. (2002) 'Management of the problem', in Smith, S.M. (ed.) *The maltreatment of children*. Lancaster: MTP, pp. 83-95.

1.7 Multi-volume works

Citation order:

- Author or editor
- Year of publication (in round brackets)
- Title of book (in italics)
- Volumes (in round brackets)
- Place of publication: Publisher

Example

In-text citation:

Butcher's (1961) guide ...

Reference list:

Butcher, R. (1961) *A new British flora*. (2 vols.) London: Leonard Hill.

Citing a single volume of a multi-volume work

Add the title of the relevant volume to your reference list.

Example

In-text citation:

Part 1 of Butcher's work (1961) …

Reference list:

Butcher, R. (1961) *A new British flora. Part 1: lycopodiaceae to salicaceae*. London: Leonard Hill.

1.8 Chapters in multi-volume works

Citation order:

* Author of the chapter/section (surname followed by initials)
* Year of publication (in round brackets)
* Title of chapter/section (in single quotation marks)
* 'in' plus author/editor of book
* Title of book (in italics)
* Place of publication: Publisher
* Page numbers of chapter/section

Example

In-text citation:

In analysing ports (Jackson, 2000) …

Reference list:

Jackson, G. (2000) 'Ports 1700-1840', in Clark, P. (ed.) *Cambridge urban history of Britain: Vol. 2 1540-1840*. Cambridge: Cambridge University Press, pp.705-731.

1.9 Reference books

In many cases reference material (e.g. encyclopaedias, bibliographies) does not have an obvious author or editor, and is usually known and therefore cited by its title.

Citation order:

As for **1.1 Information in books**

Example: with author

In-text citation:

Beal (2008, p.171) identified …

Reference list:

Beal, P. (2008) 'Folio', *A dictionary of English manuscript terminology: 1450 to 2000*. Oxford: Oxford University Press.

Example: with no author

In-text citation:

The definition (*Collins beginner's German dictionary*, 2008, p.21) …

Reference list:

Collins beginner's German dictionary (2008) New York: Collins.

1.10 Online reference books

As with other print sources, a growing number of reference books are now available as e-books. There are two examples given below. The first is an example of a print book made available online. The second is an example of a reference work that was published in print and online. The online version is being

Harvard referencing style

updated regularly; the print version will not be updated until a new edition is published. As with other examples where print and online versions exist, be careful to reference the version you have used as this example shows how they can vary.

Citation order:

As for **1.6 Chapters/sections of edited books** but replace Place of publication: Publisher with [Online] Available at: URL (Accessed: date)

Example

In-text citation:

The process of adaptation is difficult to detect (Rose, 2007, p.19).

Reference list:

Rose, M.R. (2007) 'Adaptation' in Levin, S.A. (ed.) *Encyclopedia of biodiversity*, pp.17-23 [Online] Available at: http://www.sciencedirect.com/science/referenceworks/9780122268656 (Accessed: 5 June 2008).

Example of printed reference work that is being updated online:

In-text citation for print version:

Rutherford's contribution (Badash, 2004)…

Reference list for print version:

Badash, L. (2004) 'Rutherford, Ernest, Baron Rutherford of Nelson (1871-1937)', in *Oxford dictionary of national biography*. Oxford: Oxford University Press, pp. 381-389.

In-text citation for online version:

Rutherford's contribution (Badash, 2008) …

Reference list for online version (which is being updated but print is not):

Badash, L. (2008) 'Rutherford, Ernest, Baron Rutherford of Nelson (1871-1937)', in *Oxford dictionary of national biography*, (2004) [Online]. Available at http://www.oxforddnb.com/view/article/35891 (Accessed: 25 June 2008).

1.11 Atlases (see also 18.4 Maps)

Citation order:

As for **1.1 Information in books**

Example

In-text citation:

As illustrated in the text (*The Times atlas of the world*, 2002, p.201) …

Reference list:

The Times atlas of the world (2002) London: Times Books.

1.12 Audiobooks

Citation order:

As for **20.4 Music or spoken word recordings on audio CDs/audio CD-ROMs** and **20.5 Music or spoken word recordings on audio cassettes**

1.13 Pamphlets

Citation order:

As for **1.1 Information in books**

Example

In-text citation:

Bradley's pamphlet (1994) gave instructions in the use of …

Reference list:

Bradley, M. (1994) *CD-ROMs: how to set up your workstation*. London: ASLIB.

1.14 Exhibition catalogues

Citation order:

- Author of catalogue
- Year (in round brackets)
- Title of exhibition (in italics)
- Location and date(s) of exhibition
- [Exhibition catalogue]

Example

In-text citation:

Urbach (2007, p.8) noted the demands for reform …

Reference list:

Urbach, P. (2007) *Reform! Reform! Reform!* Exhibition held at the Reform Club, London 2005-2006 and at Grey College, Durham University, March 2007 [Exhibition catalogue].

1.15 Anthologies

1.15a Citation order:

- Editor/compiler of anthology (surname followed by initials)
- Year of publication (in round brackets)
- Title of book (in italics)
- Place of publication: Publisher

Example

In-text citation:

In his collection of humorous poems, West (1989) …

Reference list:

West, C. (compiler and illustrator) (1989) *The beginner's book of bad behaviour*. London: Beaver Books.

1.15b Citation order for line of a poem within an anthology:

- Author of the poem (surname followed by initials)
- Year of publication (in round brackets)
- Title of poem (in single quotation marks)
- 'in' plus author/editor/compiler of book
- Title of book (in italics)
- Place of publication: Publisher
- Page reference

Example

In-text citation:

"The lion made a sudden stop
He let the dainty morsel drop"
(Belloc,1989, p.89).

Reference list:

Belloc, H. (1989) 'Jim', in West, C. (compiler and illustrator) *The beginner's book of bad behaviour*. London: Beaver Books, pp. 88-92.

1.16 Lines within a play

Citation order:

- Author (surname followed by initials)
- Year of publication (in round brackets)
- Title (in italics)
- Edition information
- Place of publication: Publisher
- Act. Scene: line

Example

In-text citation:

"I prithee do not mock me fellow student" (Shakespeare, 1980, I.2:177).

Reference list:

Shakespeare, W. (1980) *Hamlet*. Edited by Spencer, T.J.B. London: Penguin. I.2:177.

NB. If citing from a live performance, see **19.3 Plays.**

1.17 Sacred texts

1.17a The Bible

There is a well-established system for citing references from the Bible in your text. This uses the book name, chapter and verse (not page number, as this will vary between printings). It also avoids stating authors, as the actual authorship of some books is unclear.

Citation order:

- Book of the Bible
- Chapter: verse
- Version of the Bible (not in italics)

Example

In-text citation:

The Beatitudes (Matthew 5: 3-12) ...

Reference list:

- Add the version of the Bible you have read
- Publisher and publication date are not required, for example:

Matthew 5: 3-12, Revised Standard Version of the Bible.

1.17b. The Torah

Citation order:

- Torah (not in italics)
- Book
- Chapter: verse

Example

In-text citation:

The reply (Shemot 3:14) is the most profound …

Reference list:

Torah. Shemot 3:14.

Example

In-text citation:

Ushpol (1958) noted the key research …

Reference list:

Ushpol, R. (1958) *Select bibliography of South African autobiographies*. Cape Town: University of Cape Town, School of Librarianship.

1.17c. The Qur'an

Citation order:

- Qu'ran (not in italics)
- Surah (or Chapter): verse

Example

In-text citation:

"They are your brethren in faith" (Qur'an 9:11).

Reference list:

Qur'an 9:11.

1.18 Bibliographies

Although print bibliographies have been largely replaced by electronic databases for current information, they may provide commentary and highlight earlier sources not covered by modern databases.

2. Journal articles

2.1 Articles in printed journals

Citation order:

- Author (surname followed by initials)
- Year of publication (in round brackets)
- Title of article (in single quotation marks)
- Title of journal (in italics - capitalise first letter of each word in title, except for linking words such as and, of, the, for)
- Issue information (volume, part number, month or season)
- Page reference

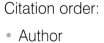

Example

In-text citation:

… the customer playing the part of a partial employee (Dawes and Rowley, 1998, p.352).

Reference list:

Dawes, J. and Rowley, J. (1998) 'Enhancing the customer experience: contributions from information technology', *Management Decision*, 36 (5), pp. 350-357.

2.2 Journal articles in online collections (e-journals)

The great majority of electronic journals available through library web pages are part of journal collections, e.g. *Ebsco, Ingenta, Emerald, Infotrac, JSTOR, Proquest, ScienceDirect*. You should refer to the fact that you obtained the title online, because online versions sometimes omit sections found in the printed version, such as advertisements and letters from readers.

Citation order:

- Author
- Year of publication (in round brackets)
- Title of article (in single quotation marks)
- Title of journal (in italics - capitalise first letter of each word in title, except for linking words such as and, of, the, for)
- Volume, issue, page numbers
- Name of collection (in italics)
- [Online]
- Available at: URL of collection or Digital Object Identifier (see **p.21**) and example over the page
- (Accessed: date)

Example: with one author

In-text citation:

Bright (1985, p.269) found the word 'poetry' ambiguous …

Reference list:

Bright, M. (1985) 'The poetry of art', *Journal of the History of Ideas*, 46 (2), pp. 259-277 *JSTOR* [Online]. Available at: http://uk.jstor.org/ (Accessed: 16 June 2008).

Example: with multiple authors

In-text citation:

A review by Liu *et al.* (2008) …

Reference list:

Liu, B.C., Ivers, R., Norton, R., Boufous, S., Blows, S. and Lo, S.K. (2008) 'Review of professional training', *Cochrane Database of Systematic Reviews*, 2, *Ovid* [Online]. Available at: http://ovidsp.uk.ovid.com/spb/ovidweb.cgi (Accessed: 23 June 2008)..

Example: article with Digital Object Identifier (DOI)

In-text citation:

Observations by Horsh *et al.* (2008) …

Reference list:

Horsh, E.P., van Altena, W.F., Cyr, W.M., Kinsman-Smith, L., Srivastava, A. and Zhou, J. (2008) 'Charge-coupled device speckle observations of binary stars with the WIYN telescope. V. Measures during 2001-2006', *Astronomical Journal*, 136, pp. 312-322. [Online] DOI: 10.1088/0004-6256/136/1/312 (Accessed: 7 July 2008).

Example

In-text citation:

… whilst Pauli (2008) reported …

Reference list:

Pauli, M.. (2008) 'Libraries of the future', *Ariadne*, 55, April [Online]. Available at: http://www.ariadne.ac.uk/issue55/jisc-debates-rpt/ (Accessed: 16 June 2008).

2.3 Articles in Internet journals (e-journals)

There are a growing number of journals that are published solely on the Internet, with no printed issue available.

Citation order:

* Author
* Year of publication (in round brackets)
* Title of article (in single quotation marks)
* Title of journal (in italics and capitalise first letter of each word in title, except for linking words such as and, of, the, for)
* Volume, issue or month/season
* [Online]
* Available at: URL of web page
* (Accessed: date)

2.4 Articles in open access journals (e-journals)

The Internet provides a means for high quality academic research to be made available to scholars in open access archives without the involvement of commercial publishers, who often charge educational institutions to access the research. Check the website to see that the journal is **peer-reviewed** (see **Glossary**) or edited by academic experts who have checked the accuracy of the research.

Citation order:

* Author
* Year (in round brackets)
* Title of article (in single quotation marks)
* Title of journal (in italics - capitalise first letter of each word in title, except for linking words such as and, of, the, for)
* Volume, issue numbers and page numbers if known
* Name of open access archive (in italics - capitalise first letter of each word in title, except for linking words such as and, of, the, for)
* [Online]
* Available at: URL
* (Accessed: date)

Example

In-text citation:

Zhang, Pare and Sandford (2008) provided an update.

Reference list:

Zhang, J., Pare, P.D. and Sandford, A. (2008) 'Recent advances in asthma genetics', *Respiratory Research*, 9(4), *BioMed Central* [Online]. Available at: http://respiratory-research.com/content /9/1/4 (Accessed: 4 July 2008).

3. Newspaper articles

3.1 Printed newspapers

Where the author of a newspaper article is identified, use the following citation order:

* Author
* Year of publication (in round brackets)
* Title of article (in single quotation marks)
* Title of newspaper (in italics - capitalise first letter of each word in title, except for linking words such as and, of, the, for)
* Edition if required (in round brackets)
* Day and month
* Page reference

Example

In-text citation:

House prices fell by 2.1% last month (Old, 2008).

Reference list:

Old, D. (2008) 'House price gloom', *Evening Chronicle* (Newcastle edn.), 26 June, p.25.

When citing a regional newspaper include the edition to distinguish it from others with the same title.

Where no author is given, use the following citation order:

* Title of newspaper (in italics- capitalise first letter of each word in title, except for linking words such as and, of, the, for)
* Year of publication (in round brackets)
* Title of article (in single quotation marks)
* Day and month
* Page reference

Example

In-text citation:

The article (*The Times*, 2008, p.7) reported ...

Reference list:

The Times (2008) 'Bank accounts', 14 June, p.7.

Note: If you are citing several articles published in the same year use a, b, c, etc after the year, e.g.

The Times (2008a) ...

3.2 Articles from Internet newspapers

Many printed newspapers produce Internet editions. These are often selections of stories from the printed source and may exclude some material or add other features. You should therefore use [Online] to make it clear that you have used the Internet version.

Citation order:

- Author
- Year of publication (in round brackets)
- Title of article (in single quotation marks)
- Title of newspaper (in italics - capitalise first letter of each word in title, except for linking words such as and, of, the, for)
- Day and month
- [Online]
- Available at: URL
- (Accessed: date)

Example

In-text citation:

Financial incentives were offered to graduates (Mansell and Bloom, 2008).

Reference list:

Mansell, W. and Bloom, A. (2008) '£8,000 carrot to tempt maths experts', *Times Educational Supplement*, 20 June [Online]. Available at: http://www.tes.co.uk/2635138 (Accessed: 23 June 2008).

3.3 Journal/newspaper articles from full-text CD-ROM databases

Citation order:

- Author
- Year of publication (in round brackets)
- Title of article (in single quotation marks)
- Journal/newspaper title (in italics - capitalise first letter of each word in title, except for linking words such as and, of, the, for)
- Volume, date (day/month), page references
- [CD-ROM]

- Producer (where identifiable)
- Available: Publisher/Distributor.

Example

In-text citation:

The political situation had a detrimental impact on oil exports (Lascelles, 1999, p.18).

Reference list:

Lascelles, D. (1999) 'Oil's troubled waters', *Financial Times*, 11 January, p.18 [CD-ROM]. Financial Times. Available: Chadwyck Healey.

4. Conferences

4.1 Full conference proceedings

Citation order:

- Author/editor
- Year of publication (in round brackets)
- Title of conference: subtitle (in italics)
- Location and date of conference
- Place of publication: Publisher

Example

In-text citation:

The conference (Institute for Small Business Affairs, 2000) …

Reference list:

Institute for Small Business Affairs (2000) *Small firms: adding the spark: the 23rd ISBA national small firms policy and research conference*. Robert Gordon University, Aberdeen 15-17 November. Leeds: Institute for Small Business Affairs.

4.2 Individual conference papers

Citation order:

- Author of paper
- Year of publication (in round brackets)
- Title of paper (in single quotation marks)
- Title of conference: subtitle (in italics)
- Location and date of conference
- Place of publication: Publisher
- Page references for the paper

Example

In-text citation:

Cook (2000) highlighted examples …

Reference list:

Cook, D. (2000) 'Developing franchised business in Scotland', *Small firms: adding the spark: the 23rd ISBA national small firms policy and research conference.* Robert Gordon University, Aberdeen 15-17 November. Leeds: Institute for Small Business Affairs, pp. 127-136.

4.3 Papers from conference proceedings published on the Internet

Citation order:

- Author
- Year of publication (in round brackets)
- Title of paper (in single quotation marks)
- Title of conference: subtitle (in italics)
- Location and date of conference
- Publisher
- Available at: URL
- (Accessed: date)

Example

In-text citation:
A recent paper (Lord, 2002) …

Reference list:

Lord, J. (2002) 'What do consumers say?' *Changing attitudes, changing strategies: reaching China's dynamic consumer markets. American Chamber of Commerce in Shanghai conference*, Shanghai 15th October. AMCHAM-Shanghai. Available at: http://www.amcham-shanghai.org/add-ons/marketing-conference/default.aspx (Accessed: 8 August 2003).

5. Theses

Citation order:

- Author
- Year of submission (in round brackets)
- Title of thesis (in italics)
- Degree statement
- Degree-awarding body

5.1 Unpublished theses

Example

In-text citation:

Research by Tregear (2001) …

Reference list:

Tregear, A.E.J. (2001) *Speciality regional foods in the UK: an investigation from the perspectives of marketing and social history.* Unpublished PhD thesis. University of Newcastle upon Tyne.

5.2 Theses available on the Internet

> **Example**
>
> **In-text citation:**
>
> Research by Winkelman (2001) …
>
> **Reference list:**
>
> Winkelman, P. (2001) *Beyond science: an exploration of values in engineering education and practice*. PhD thesis. University of Calgary, Alberta [Online]. Available at: http://www.collectionscanada.gc.ca/obj/s4/f2/dsk3/ftp04/nq64892.pdf (Accessed: 14 June 2008).

- Available at: URL of Virtual Learning Environment
- (Accessed: date)

> **Example**
>
> **In-text citation:**
>
> The need for preparation (Hollis, 2008) …
>
> **Reference list:**
>
> Hollis, K. (2008) 'Week 7: dissertation preparation materials'. *Research methods for MA History* [Online]. Available at: http://duo.dur.ac.uk (Accessed: 2 February 2008).

6. Virtual Learning Environments (e.g. Blackboard, WebCT)

Virtual Learning Environments (e.g. Blackboard and WebCT) are used in further and higher education as stores for course documents and teaching materials, and for discussion between tutors and students and between students. You will need to distinguish what you are citing, for example a tutor's notes, a journal article, text extracted from a book and digitised for use in VLEs, or an item from a discussion board. Note in the examples below that the URL is for the access point to the VLE as a reader would need login details to locate the item being cited.

6.1 Tutors' notes

Citation order:

- Author or tutor
- Year of publication (in round brackets)
- Title of item (in single quotation marks)
- Name of academic module (in italics)
- [Online]

6.2 Journal articles

Citation order:

- Author
- Year of publication (in round brackets)
- Title of article (in single quotation marks)
- Title of journal (in italics)
- Volume, issue, page numbers
- Name of academic module (in italics)
- [Online]
- Available at: URL of Virtual Learning Environment
- (Accessed: date)

> **Example**
>
> **In-text citation:**
>
> Bright (2003, p.262) believed …
>
> **Reference list:**
>
> Bright, M. (2003) 'The advance of learning', *Journal of Ideas*, 46 (2), pp. 259-277. *E-learning in the classroom* [Online]. Available at: http://duo.dur.ac.uk (Accessed: 23 July 2007).

6.3 Text extracts from books digitised for use in Virtual Learning Environments

Citation order:

- Author
- Year of publication of book (in round brackets)
- Extract title (in single quotation marks)
- In
- Title of book (in italics)
- Place of publication: Publisher (if available)
- Page numbers of extract
- Name of academic module (in italics)
- [Online]
- Available at: URL of Virtual Learning Environment
- (Accessed: date)

Example

In-text citation:

At least one author (Fenwick, 2007) …

Reference list:

Fenwick, H. (2007). 'The Human Rights Act', in *Civil liberties and human rights*. London: Routledge Cavendish, pp.157-298. *Legal skills* [Online]. Available at: http://duo.dur.ac.uk (Accessed: 7 June 2008).

6.4 Messages from course discussion boards

Citation order:

- Author
- Year of publication (in round brackets)
- Title of message (in single quotation marks)
- Title of discussion board (in italics)
- In

- Name of academic module (in italics)
- [Online]
- Available at: URL of Virtual Learning Environment
- (Accessed: date)

Example

In-text citation:

It is advisable to check which referencing style is required (Thomas, 2003).

Reference list:

Thomas, D. (2008) 'Word count and referencing style', *Frequently Asked Questions discussion board* in *Housing Studies* [Online]. Available at: http://duo.dur.ac.uk (Accessed: 14 May 2008).

7. Preprints or eprints

Many academic institutions maintain digital repositories of the research undertaken by their staff and make digital copies (eprints) of book chapters, journal articles and conference papers available via the Internet. If these are available before the item has been **peer-reviewed** (see **Glossary**) they are known as preprints. If they are made available after peer-review they are called postprints. Preprints and postprints are both forms of eprints. They are very useful sources of new research and are often heavily cited in scientific literature. As with all Internet-based sources, be clear what you are referencing. If it is a publication, include all information that you would if referencing the printed source, as in the book example below. If it is a prepublication article, conference, working paper or presentation that has not been peer-reviewed or formatted by publishers, or is a draft of work that was published later, be clear that you are referencing the preprint.

7.1 Books in digital repositories

Citation order:

- Author
- Year (in round brackets)
- Title (in italics)
- Place of publication: Publisher (if stated)
- Name of digital repository (in italics)
- [Online]
- Available at: URL
- (Accessed: date)

Example

In-text citation:

Previous PhD candidates provided useful advice (Cook and Crang, 1995).

Reference list:

Cook, I. and Crang, M. (1995) *Doing ethnographies*. Norwich: Geobooks. *Durham Research Online* [Online]. Available at: http://dro.dur.ac.uk/202/ (Accessed: 29 June 2008).

7.2 Pre-publication journal articles in digital repositories

Citation order:

- Author
- Year (in round brackets)
- Title of article (in single quotation marks)
- To be published in (if this is stated)
- Title of journal (in italics and capitalise first letter of each word in title, except for linking words such as and, of, the, for)
- Volume and issue numbers (if stated)
- Name of repository (in italics)
- [Preprint]
- Available at: URL
- (Accessed: date)

Example

In-text citation:

Canal surface research by Dohm and Zube (2008) ...

Reference list:

Dohm, M. and Zube, S. (2008) 'The implicit equation of a canal surface'. To be published in *Journal of Symbolic Computation. Arxiv* [Preprint]. Available at: http://arxiv.org/abs/0806.4127v1 (Accessed: 29 June 2008).

7.3 Conference papers in digital repositories

Citation order:

- Author
- Year of publication (in round brackets)
- Title of paper (in single quotation marks)
- Title of conference: subtitle (in italics)
- Organisation or company (if stated)
- Location and date of conference
- Name of repository (in italics)
- [Online]
- Available at: URL
- (Accessed: date)

Example

In-text citation:

Price (2001) disputed the theory ...

Reference list:

Price, P. B. (2001) 'Life in solid ice?' *Workshop on life in ancient ice*, Westin Salishan Lodge, Gleneden Beach, Oregon, 30 June - 2 July 2001. *Arxiv* [Online]. Available at: http://arxiv.org/abs/q-bio/0507004 (Accessed: 30 June 2008).

8. The Internet

When referencing information you have retrieved from the Internet **you must distinguish what you are referring to**. The Internet is made up of journal articles, organisation Internet sites, personal Internet sites, government publications, images, company data, presentations - a vast range of material. Examples of how to reference individual sources, such as journal articles, e-books and images, are given with the entries for those sources. You will find below examples of how to cite and reference Internet sites or web pages produced by individuals and organisations. The nature of what you are referring to will govern how you cite or reference it. You should aim to provide all of the data that a reader would require to locate your information source. As material on the Internet can be removed or changed, you should also note the date when you accessed/viewed the information - it might not be there in a few months time! Remember to evaluate all Internet information for accuracy, authority, currency, coverage and objectivity. The ability to publish information on the Internet bears no relation to the author's academic abilities!

The defining element in referencing a web page is its Uniform Resource Locator, or URL. This should be included in your reference list, but do not include the URL in your in-text citation, unless this is the only piece of information you have.

Citing and referencing organisation or personal web pages

8.1 Web pages with individual authors

Citation order:

- Author
- Year that the site was published/last updated (in round brackets)
- Title of Internet site (in italics)
- Available at: URL
- (Accessed: date)

Example

In-text citation:

Yau (2001) provided information about the Chinese community.

Reference list:

Yau, T. (2001) *Dragon project*. Available at: http://www.geocities.com/dragonproject2000/ (Accessed: 14 June 2008).

8.2 Web pages with organisations as authors

Example

In-text citation:

The *Open gardens* scheme (British Red Cross, 2008) …

Reference list:

British Red Cross (2008) *Open gardens*. Available at: http://www.redcross.org.uk/index.asp?id=39992 (Accessed: 17 June 2008).

8.3 Web pages with no authors

Use the title of the site.

> **Example**
>
> **In-text citation:**
>
> Illustrations of the houses can be found online (*Palladio's Italian villas*, 2005).
>
> **Reference list:**
>
> *Palladio's Italian villas* (2005) Available at: http://www.boglewood.com/palladio/ (Accessed: 2 June 2008).

8.4 Web pages with no authors or titles

If no author or title can be identified, you should use the site's URL. It may be possible to truncate a very long URL, so long as the route remains clear, but it may be necessary to give the full URL even in your text. If a web page has no author or title you might question whether or not it is suitable for academic work.

> **Example**
>
> **In-text citation:**
>
> Video files may need to be compressed (http://www.newmediarepublic.com/dvideo /compression.html, 2008).
>
> **Reference list:**
>
> http://www.newmediarepublic.com/dvideo/ compression.html (2008) (Accessed: 14 June 2008).

8.5 Web pages with no dates

If the web page has no obvious date of publication/revision, use the URL (no date) and the date you accessed the page. You might question how useful undated information is to your research as it may be out of date!

> **Example**
>
> **In-text citation:**
>
> Compression may be required (http://www.newmediarepublic.com/dvideo /compression.html, no date).
>
> **Reference list:**
>
> http://www.newmediarepublic.com/dvideo/ compression.html (no date) (Accessed: 14 June 2008).

8.6 Blogs

Weblogs, or 'blogs' as they are usually called, are produced by individuals and organisations to provide updates on issues of interest or concern. Beware that as blogs are someone's opinions they may not provide objective, reasoned discussion of an issue. Use blogs in conjunction with reputable sources. Note that due to the informality of the Internet, many authors give first names or aliases. Use the name they have used in your reference.

Citation order:

- Author of message
- Year that the site was published/last updated (in round brackets)
- Title of message (in single quotation marks)
- Title of Internet site (in italics)
- Day/month of posted message
- Available at: URL
- (Accessed: date)

Example

In-text citation:

Nick Robinson (2008) noted the "Cameron Direct" phenomenon.

Reference list:

Robinson, N. (2008) 'Cameron Direct', *Nick Robinson's newslog*, 4 June. Available at: http://www.bbc.co.uk/blogs/nickrobinson/ (Accessed: 11 June 2008).

Example

In-text citation:

Telford introduced new techniques of bridge construction ('Thomas Telford', 2008).

Reference list:

'Thomas Telford' (2008) *Wikipedia*. Available at: http://en.wikipedia.org/wiki/Thomas_Telford (Accessed: 11 June 2008).

8.7 Wikis

Wikis are collaborative websites in which several (usually unidentified) authors can add and edit the information presented. What you read today may have changed by tomorrow. There have also been instances of false information being presented, though wiki editors try to ensure that the information is authentic. If you are going to use information from a wiki, **make sure that it is thoroughly referenced**. As with other websites, if there are no authors or references given the information is unlikely to be suitable for academic work. Evaluate wiki information against sources of proven academic quality such as books and journal articles.

Citation order:

- Title of article (in single quotation marks)
- Year that the site was published/last updated (in round brackets)
- Title of Internet site (in italics)
- Available at: URL
- (Accessed: date)

8.8 Social networking websites (e.g. *Facebook, Bebo, Friends Reunited*)

These are web pages and can be referenced as such. Note that as these sites require registration and then acceptance of friendship by other members, it is suggested that the main web address be used. You may wish to include a copy of the member-to-member discussion you are referring to as an appendix to your work, so that readers without access to the original can read it.

Citation order:

- Author
- Year that the site was published/last updated (in round brackets)
- Title of page (in single quotation marks)
- Title of Internet site (in italics)
- Day/month of posted message
- Available at: URL
- (Accessed: date)

Example

In-text citation:

One student (Thomas, 2008) sent his contribution from Paris.

Reference list:

Thomas, J. (2008) 'Northumbria Group', *Facebook*, 3 June. Available at: http://www.facebook.com (Accessed: 13 June 2008).

9. CD-ROMs or DVD-ROMs

Citation order:

- Title of publication (in italics)
- Year of publication (in round brackets)
- [CD-ROM] or [DVD-ROM]
- Producer (where identifiable)
- Available: Publisher/Distributor

Example

In-text citation:

The student made extensive use of an authoritative source (*World development indicators*, 2002) …

Reference list:

World development indicators (2002) [CD-ROM]. The World Bank Group. Available: SilverPlatter.

10. Computer programs

Citation order:

- Author (if given)
- Date (if given)
- Title of program (in italics and capitalise)
- Version (in round brackets)

- Form i.e. Computer program (in square brackets)
- Availability i.e. Distributor, address, order number (if given) **OR** URL if downloaded from the Internet

Example

In-text citation:

Camtasia Studio (TechSmith, 2008) can be used to record tutorials.

Reference list:

TechSmith Corporation (2008) *Camtasia Studio* (Version 3) [Computer program]. Available at: http://www.techsmith.com/download/trials. asp (Accessed: 21 June 2008).

11. Reports

Citation order:

- Author or organisation
- Year of publication (in round brackets)
- Title of report (in italics)
- Place of publication: Publisher

  OR if accessed on the Internet:
- [Online]
- Available at: URL
- (Accessed: date)

Harvard referencing style

11.1 Research reports

Example

In-text citation:

The minimum cost of living in Britain is £13,400 (Bradshaw *et al.*, 2008, p.32).

Reference list:

Bradshaw, J., Middleton, S., Davis, A., Oldfield, N., Smith, N., Cusworth, L. and Williams, J. (2008) *A minimum income standard for Britain: what people think.* [Online]. Available at: http://www.jrf.org.uk/bookshop/eBooks/2226-income-poverty-standards.pdf (Accessed: 3 July 2008).

11.2 Company annual reports

Example

In-text citation:

The company's profits expanded (British Sky Broadcasting Group plc, 2007) ...

Reference list:

British Sky Broadcasting Group plc (2007) *Annual report* [Online]. Available at: http://library.corporate-ir.net/library/10/104/104016/items/258443/AR07.pdf (Accessed: 3 July 2008).

11.3 Market research reports from online databases

Example

In-text citation:

Mintel (2008) noted problems in the market ...

Reference list:

Mintel (2008) 'Car insurance UK', *Mintel oxygen reports platform* [Online]. Available at: http://academic.mintel.com (Accessed: 5 July 2008).

NB The section of the report collection is given in single quotation marks.

11.4 Financial reports from online databases

Citation order:

- Publishing organisation
- Year of publication/last updated (in round brackets)
- Title of extract (in single quotation marks)
- Database title (in italics)
- [Online]
- Available at: URL
- (Accessed: date)

Example

In-text citation:

"BT's profit margin rose by over 2% in the financial year 2006-2007 (Bureau van Dijk, 2008)."

Reference list:

Bureau van Dijk (2008) 'BT Group plc company report', *FAME* [Online]. Available at: http://fame.bvdep.com (Accessed: 2 July 2008).

Harvard referencing style

12 Legal material using the Harvard (author-date) style

In many instances there are established guidelines for referencing legal material which are different to the procedures used in Harvard style. Some examples of how to cite and reference legal sources in Harvard style are given below. For other legal sources refer to the examples in **Section E1: OSCOLA referencing style**.

12.1 House of Commons and House of Lords Papers

Citation order:

- Great Britain

- Parliament. House of...

- Year of publication (in round brackets)

- Title (in italics)

- Place of publication: Publisher

- Paper number (in brackets). For House of Lords papers the paper number is also in round brackets to distinguish it from identical House of Commons paper numbers (see example below)

Examples

In-text citation:

Parliamentary reports for the year included the criminal justice system (Great Britain. Parliament. House of Commons, 1999) and renewable energy (Great Britain. Parliament. House of Lords, 1999).

Reference list:

Great Britain. Parliament. House of Commons. (1999) *Criminal justice: working together*, Session 1999-2000. London:The Stationery Office. (HC 1999-2000 29).

Great Britain. Parliament. House of Lords. (1999) *Electricity from renewables: first report from the Select Committee on the European Union*. London: The Stationery Office. (HL 1999-2000 (18)).

12.2 Bills (either House of Commons or House of Lords)

Citation order:

- Great Britain

- Parliament. House of...

- Year of publication (in round brackets)

- Title (in italics)

- Place of publication: Publisher

- Bill number (in brackets)

Example

In-text citation:

Haulage companies expressed concern about the provisions of the *Transport Bill* (Great Britain. Parliament. House of Commons, 1999).

Reference list:

Great Britain. Parliament. House of Commons. (1999) *Transport Bill*. London: The Stationery Office. (Bills 1999-2000 8).

12.3 UK Statutes (Acts of Parliament)

A major change in the citation of UK legal sources took place in 1963. Before this, an Act was cited according to the regnal year (i.e. the number of years since the monarch's accession).

For pre-1963 statutes use

Citation order:

- Short title of Act and year (in italics)
- Regnal year
- Name of sovereign
- Chapter number

Example: pre-1963 Act

In-text citation:

With the *Act of Supremacy 1534* (26 Hen.8, c.1) ...

Reference list:

Act of Supremacy 1534 (26 Hen.8, c.1)

For post-1963 statutes use the short title of an Act, with the year in which it was enacted.

Citation Order:

- Great Britain
- Name of Act: Name of sovereign. Chapter number (in italics)
- Year of publication (in round brackets)
- Place of publication: Publisher

Example: post-1963 Act

In-text citation:

The statute (Great Britain. *Access to Justice Act 1999*) laid down ...

Reference list:

Great Britain. *Access to Justice Act 1999: Elizabeth II. Chapter 22*. (1999) London: The Stationery Office.

Example: section of an Act

In-text citation:

Authority, as defined in s.10(4)(6) of the Act (Great Britain. *Children Act 2004*) ...

Reference list:

Great Britain. *Children Act 2004: Elizabeth II. Chapter 31*. London: The Stationery Office.

12.4 Statutory Instruments

Citation order:

- Name/title including year (in italics)
- SI year and number (in round brackets)

Example

In-text citation:

The *Terrorism (United Nations Measures) Order 2001* ...

Reference list:

Terrorism (United Nations Measures) Order 2001 (SI 2001/3365).

Harvard referencing style

13. Government publications

These include Green and White Papers (published as Command Papers) which propose policies, and publications by individual departments giving advice or information.

13.1 Command Papers including Green and White Papers

Citation order:

* Great Britain
* Name of Committee or Royal Commission
* Year of publication (in round brackets)
* Title (in italics)
* Place of publication: Publisher
* Paper number (in brackets)

Example

In-text citation:

The latest advice (Great Britain. Lord Chancellor's Department, 1999) …

Reference list:

Great Britain. Lord Chancellor's Department (1999) *Government policy on archives*. London: The Stationery Office. (Cm. 4516).

13.2 Departmental publications

Citation order:

* Country
* Name of government department
* Year of publication (in round brackets)
* Title (in italics)
* Place of publication: Publisher
* Series (in brackets) - if applicable

If referencing an online version replace Place of publication: Publisher with:

* [Online]
* Available at: URL
* (Accessed: date)

Examples

In-text citations:

Prison numbers increased last year (Great Britain. Ministry of Justice, 2007) as did the disparity in medical care (Great Britain. Department of Health, 2008; 2004).

Reference list:

Great Britain. Department of Health (2004) *Primary medical services allocations 2004/05*. Health Service Circular HSC 2004/003 [Online]. Available at: http://www.dh.gov.u/en/Publicationsandstatistics/Lettersandcirculars/Healthservicecirculars/DH_4071269 (Accessed: 21 June 2008).

Great Britain. Department of Health (2008) *Health inequalities: progress and next steps* [Online]. Available at: http://www.dh.gov.uk/en/Publicationsandstatistics/Publications/PublicationsPolicyAndGuidance/DH_085307 (Accessed: 18 June 2008).

Great Britain. Ministry of Justice (2007) *Sentencing statistics* (*annual*) [Online]. Available at: http://www.justice.gov.uk/publications/sentencingannual.htm (Accessed: 3 June 2008).

It is important to include the country of origin as publications from many governments are available on the Internet:

Example

In-text citation:

One country which has taken a tough stance is Canada (Canada. Department of Foreign Affairs and International Trade, 2001).

Reference list:

Canada. Department of Foreign Affairs and International Trade (2001) *Re-affirming the commitment: 2000-2001 report on the Canadian Landmine Fund* [Online]. Available at: http://www.dfait-maeci.gc.ca/foreign_policy/mines/ar-00-01-en.asp (Accessed: 3 July 2008).

14. Publications of international organisations

Citation order:

- Name of organisation or institution
- Year of publication (in round brackets)
- Title (in italics)
- Place of publication: Publisher

Example

In-text citation:

A report by the United Nations (2005) …

Reference list:

United Nations (2005) *Yearbook of the United Nations, 2003 vol. 57*. New York: United Nations Department of Public Information.

NB If you have retrieved a document from the Internet, omit the place of publication and add the following to the citation order:

- [Online]
- Available at: URL
- (Accessed: date)

Example

In-text citation:

At least one transport organisation (International Chamber of Commerce, Commission for Air Transport, 2000) …

Reference list:

International Chamber of Commerce, Commission for Air Transport (2000) *The need for greater liberalization in international air transport*. International Chamber of Commerce (310/504 Rev.3) [Online]. Available at: http://www.iccwbo.org/home/statements_rules/statements/2000/need_for_greater_liberalization.asp (Accessed: 9 Feb 2005).

15. European Union publications

Citation order:

- Name of EU Institution (e.g. Council of the European Union, European Commission)
- Year of publication (in round brackets)
- Title (in italics)
- Place of publication: Publisher

Example

In-text citation:

The predicted migration of labour (European Commission, 2003) …

Harvard referencing style

Reference list:

European Commission (2003) *Making globalisation work for everyone*. Luxembourg: Office for Official Publications of the European Communities.

16. Scientific and technical information

16.1 British Standards

16.1a British Standards

Citation order:

- Name of authorising organisation
- Year of publication (in round brackets)
- Number and title of standard (in italics)
- Place of publication: Publisher

Example

In-text citation:

Loft conversions are subject to strict controls (British Standards Institute, 1989).

Reference list:

British Standards Institute (1989) *BS5268-7.4: Structural use of timber: ceiling binders*. London: British Standards Institute.

16.1b British Standards from online databases

Citation order:

- Name of authorising organisation
- Year of publication (in round brackets)
- Number and title of standard (in italics)
- Title of database (in italics)
- [Online]

- Available at: URL
- (Accessed: date)

Example

In-text citation:

Standards also apply to the use of timber (British Standards Institute, 1989) …

Reference list:

British Standards Institute (1989) BS5268-7.4: *Structural use of timber: ceiling binders. StandardsUK.com* [Online]. Available at: http://www.standardsuk.com/ (Accessed: 30 June 2008).

16.2 Patents

Citation order:

- Inventor(s)
- Year of publication (in round brackets)
- Title (in italics)
- Authorising organisation
- Patent number
- [Online]
- Available at: URL
- (Accessed: date)

Example

In-text citation:

Dear (2007) proposed a solution.

Reference list:

Dear, A.G. (2007) *Plastic bag carrier*. UK Intellectual Property Office Patent no. GB2439278 [Online]. Available at: http://www.ipo.gov.uk/p-find-publication (Accessed: 1 July 2008).

16.3 Scientific datasets

Reference where you located the data, e.g. journal article/book/online.

Citation order:

- Authors
- Date (in round brackets)
- Title of data (in single quotation marks)
- Title of database(in italics)
- Version
- [Online]
- Available at: URL
- (Accessed: date)

Example

In-text citation:

The data (Ralchenko *et al*., 2008) proved …

Reference list:

Ralchenko, Y., Kramida, A.E., Reader, J., and NIST ASD Team (2008) 'Na spectrum data', *National Institute of Standards and Technology atomic spectra database* (version 3.1.5) [Online]. Available at: http://physics.nist.gov/asd3 (Accessed: 2 July 2008).

16.4 Mathematical equations

Reference where you located the equation, e.g. journal article online.

- Author
- Year of publication (in round brackets)
- Title of article (in single quotation marks)
- Title of journal (in italics and capitalise first letter of each word in title, except for linking words such as and, of, the, for)
- Volume, issue, page numbers
- [Online]
- Available at: URL of web page or DOI

- (Accessed: date)

Example

In-text citation:

Fradelizi and Meyer (2008, p.1449) noted that for z>0

$$P(K) \geqslant \frac{e^{n+1-z}z^{n+1}}{(n!)^2}$$

Reference list:

Fradelizi, M. and Meyer, M. (2008) 'Some functional inverse Santaló inequalities', *Advances in Mathematics*, 218 (5), pp.1430-1452 [Online]. DOI: 10.1016/j.aim.2008.03.013 (Accessed: 3 July 2008).

16.5 Graphs

Reference where you located the graph, e.g. graph in a book (give book details).

- Author
- Year of publication (in round brackets)
- Title of book (in italics)
- Place of publication: Publisher
- Page number or figure number for graph
- Graph

Example

In-text citation:

The effects of the compounds (Day and Gastel, 2006, p.95) …

Reference list:

Day, R. and Gastel, B. (2006) *How to write and publish a scientific paper.* Cambridge: Cambridge University Press, p.95, graph.

17. Reviews

Citation order:

- Name of the reviewer (if indicated)
- Year of publication of the review (in round brackets)
- Title of the review (in single quotation marks)
- Review of . . .
- Identification of the work reviewed (in italics)
- Author/director of work being reviewed
- Publication details (in italics)

17.1 Book reviews

Example

In-text citation:

Darden (2007) considered the book …

Reference list:

Darden, L. (2007) 'New cell research'. Review of *Discovering cell mechanisms: the creation of modern cell biology*, by William Bechtel. *Journal of the History of Biology,* 40 (1), pp.185-7.

17.2 Drama reviews

Example

In-text citation:

One reviewer (Billington, 2008, p.19) wrote…

Reference list:

Billington, M. (2008) 'The main event'. Review of *On the rocks*, by D.H. Lawrence. Hampstead Theatre, London. *The Guardian* (Review section), 5 July, p.19.

17.3 Film reviews

Example

In-text citation:

Barnes (1989) and Ward (2003) thought it a classic film.

Reference list:

Example: magazine review

Barnes, L. (1989) 'Citizen Kane'. Review of *Citizen Kane*, directed by Orson Welles. (RKO). *New Vision*, 9 October, p. 24-25.

Example: Internet review

Ward, M. (2003) 'A unique and well done movie'. Review of *Citizen Kane*, directed by Orson Welles. (RKO) *Internet movie database*. Available at: http://www.imdb.com/title/tt0033467/usercomments (Accessed: 5 July 2008).

17.4 Reviews of musical performances

Example

In-text citation:

Hickling (2008) thought it "a little touch of magic".

Reference list:

Hickling, A. (2008) 'The opera'. Review of *Don Giovanni*, by Mozart, New Vic, Newcastle-under-Lyme. *The Guardian* (Review section), 5 July, p.19.

18. Visual sources

The Internet has revolutionised the availability of visual sources such as images, maps and artistic works. Some examples below (listed in alphabetical order) will show how to cite and reference the original works and online versions.

18.1 Book illustrations, diagrams or tables

Citation order:

- Author of book
- Year of publication (in round brackets)
- Title of book (in italics)
- Place of publication: Publisher
- Page reference of illustration, etc.
- Illus./fig./table

Example

In-text citation:

Holbein's painting illustrated the prelate's ornate mitre (Strong, 1990, pp.62-3).

Reference list:

Strong, R. (1990) *Lost treasures of Britain*. London: Viking, pp.62-3, illus.

18.2 Cartoons

Citation order:

- Artist
- Date (if available)
- Title of cartoon (in single quotation marks))
- [Cartoon]
- Title of publication (in italics)

- Day and month

If seen online add:

- [Online]
- Available at: URL
- Accessed: date

Example

In-text citation:

Steve Bell (2008) warned of the danger ...

Reference list:

Bell, S. (2008) 'Don't let this happen' [Cartoon]. *The Guardian*, 19 June [Online]. Available at: http://www.guardian.co.uk/world/cartoon/2008/jun/19/steve.bell.afghanistan.troops (Accessed: 2 July 2008).

18.3 Installations

Citation order:

- Artist
- Year (in round brackets)
- Title of installation (in italics)
- [Installation]
- Location
- Date seen

Example

In-text citation:

My bed by Tracey Emin (1999) ...

Reference list:

Emin, T. (1999) *My bed* [Installation]. Tate Gallery, London, 31 October.

18.4 Maps

18.4a Ordnance Survey maps

Citation order:

- Ordnance Survey
- Year of publication (in round brackets)
- Title (in italics)
- Sheet number, scale
- Place of publication: Publisher
- Series (in brackets)

Example

In-text citation:

The landscape has undergone profound changes since the map (Ordnance Survey,1980) was printed.

Reference list:

Ordnance Survey (1980) *Bellingham, (solid)*, sheet 13, 1:50,000. Southampton: Ordnance Survey. (Geological Survey of Great Britain [England and Wales]).

Example

In-text citation:

Archaeological sites are italicised (Ordnance Survey, 2002).

Reference list:

Ordnance Survey (2002) *Preston and Blackpool*, sheet 102, 1:50,000. Southampton: Ordnance Survey. (Landranger series).

18.4b Geological Survey maps

Citation order:

- Corporate author and publisher
- Year of publication (in round brackets)
- Title (in italics)
- Sheet number, scale
- Place of publication: Publisher
- Series (in round brackets)

18.4c Online maps

Citation order:

- Map publisher
- Year of publication (in round brackets)
- Title of map section (in single quotation marks)
- Sheet number or tile, scale
- Title of online source (in italics)
- [Online]
- Available at: URL
- (Accessed: date)

Example

In-text citation:

The leisure centre is close to Tiddenfoot Lake (Ordnance Survey, 2008).

Reference list:

Ordnance Survey (2008) 'Tiddenfoot Lake', Tile sp92sw, 1:10,000. *Digimap* [Online]. Available at: http://edina.ac.uk/digimap/ (Accessed: 3 July 2008).

Harvard referencing style

Example

In-text citation:

The dock layout and road network can be seen using *Google Maps* (Tele Atlas, 2008).

Reference list:

Tele Atlas (2008) 'Cardiff Bay', *Google Maps* [Online]. Available at: http://maps.google.co.uk (Accessed: 5 July 2008).

Example: painting in online collection

In-text citation:

Dalí's *Madonna* (1958) is seated in an ear.

Reference list:

Dalí, S. (1958) *Madonna* [Oil on canvas] *Oxford art online* [Online]. Available at: http://www.oxfordartonline.com (Accessed: 9 July 2008).

18.5 Paintings/drawings

Citation order:

- Artist
- Date (if available)
- Title of the work (in italics)
- [Medium]
- Institution or collection that houses the work, followed by the city

OR if seen online:

- Name of collection (in italics)
- [Online]
- Available at:
- (Accessed: date)

Example: painting in gallery

In-text citation:

The triumph of St Augustine was one of the finest works by Coello (1664).

Reference list:

Coello, C. (1664) *The triumph of St. Augustine* [Oil on canvas]. Museo del Prado, Madrid.

18.6 Photographs

18.6a Prints or slides

Citation order:

- Photographer
- Year (in round brackets)
- Title of photograph (in italics)
- [Photograph]
- Place of publication: Publisher (if available)

Example

In-text citation:

The seasonal and architectural changes were captured on film (Thomas, 2003; Bailey, 1996).

Reference list:

Bailey, P. (1996) *Snow scene* [Photograph]. Sunderland: Centre for Visual Effects.

Thomas, T. (2003) *Redevelopment in Newcastle* [Photograph]. Newcastle upon Tyne:Then & Now Publishing.

18.6b Photographs from the Internet

Citation order:

- Photographer
- Year of publication (in round brackets)
- Title of photograph (in italics)
- [Online]
- Available at: URL
- (Accessed: date)

Example

In-text citation:

His beautiful photograph (Kitto, 2008) …

Reference list:

Kitto, J. (2008) *Golden sunset* [Online]. Available at: http://www.jameskitto.co.uk/photo_182778 6.html (Accessed: 14 June 2008).

18.6c Photographs in online collections (e.g. *Flickr*)

Citation order:

- Photographer
- Year of publication (in round brackets)
- Title of photograph (in italics)
- Title of online collection (in italics)
- [Online]
- Available at: URL
- (Accessed: date)

Example

In-text citation:

The deep hues in Kamuro's photo (2008) …

Reference list:

Kamuro (2008) *Calmness. Flickr* [Online]. Available at: http://www.flickr.com/photos/kamuro/2624 443012/in/pool-ysplix (Accessed: 30 June 2008).

18.7 Postcards

- Artist (if available)
- Date (in round brackets if available)
- Title (in italics)
- [Postcard]
- Place of publication: Publisher

Example

In-text citation:

The flat sandy beach (Corrance, no date) …

Reference list:

Corrance, D. (no date) *Gairloch, Wester Ross* [Postcard]. Scotland: Stirling Gallery.

18.8 Posters

Citation order:

- Artist (if known, or use title)
- Year (in round brackets)
- Title (in italics)
- [Poster]
- Exhibited at
- Location and date(s) of exhibition
- Dimensions (if relevant and available)

Example: poster copy of painting

In-text citation:

The image (Chagall, no date) ...

Reference list:

Chagall, M. (no date) *Le violiniste* [Poster]. 84 cm x 48cm / 33" x 19".

Example: poster for exhibition

In-text citation:

Smith's poster (2003)...

Reference list:

Smith, K. (2003) *Prints, books and things* [Poster]. Exhibited at New York, Museum of Modern Art. 5 December 2003 - 8 March 2004.

18.9 Sculpture

Citation order:

- Sculptor
- Year (in round brackets)
- Title (in italics)
- [Sculpture]
- Name of collection

Example

In-text citation:

His talents were proven with *The lovers* (Rodin, 1886).

Reference list:

Rodin, A. (1886) *The lovers*. [Sculpture]. Private collection.

If viewed online, reference the URL and date accessed.

19. Live performances

19.1 Concerts

Citation order:

- Composer
- Year of performance (in round brackets)
- Title (in italics)
- Performed by ... conducted by ...
- Location. Date seen [in square brackets]

Example

In-text citation:

A wonderful premiere (Lord, 2007) ...

Reference list:

Lord, J. (2007) *Durham Concerto.* Performed by the Liverpool Philharmonic Orchestra conducted by Mischa Damev [Durham Cathedral, Durham. 20 October].

Example: band concert

In-text citation:

The Kings of Leon (2008) wowed the crowd ...

Reference list:

Kings of Leon (2008) [Glastonbury Festival. 27 June].

19.2 Dance

Citation order:

- Composer or choreographer
- Year of premiere (in round brackets)
- Title (in italics)
- Location. Date seen [in square brackets]

Example

In-text citation:

The performance was true to the intentions of its creator (Ashton, 1937).

Reference list:

Ashton, F. (1937) *A wedding bouquet.* [Royal Opera House, London. 22 October 2004].

19.3 Plays

Citation order:

- Title (in italics)
- by Author
- Year of performance (in round brackets)
- Directed by
- Location. Date seen [in square brackets]

Example

In-text citation:

One innovation was the use of Sellotape for the fairies' webs (*A midsummer night's dream*, 1995).

Reference list:

A midsummer night's dream by William Shakespeare (1995) Directed by Ian Judge. [Theatre Royal, Newcastle upon Tyne. 26 February].

20. Audio-visual material

The Internet has radically altered access to audio and visual sources and created the means for anyone to produce and distribute material. The nature of the material and the facts necessary to identify or retrieve it should dictate the substance of your in-text citations and reference list. Examples below will cite and reference traditional and online access routes.

20.1 Radio

20.1a Radio programmes

Citation order:

- Title of programme (in italics)
- Year of transmission (in round brackets)
- Name of channel
- Date of transmission (day/month)

Example

In-text citation:

The latest report (*Today*, 2008) …

Reference list:

Today (2008) BBC Radio 4, 15 August.

20.1b Radio programmes heard on the Internet

You may listen to radio programmes live on the Internet, or days after the original transmission through services such as the BBC's Listen Again. Specify the full date of the original broadcast as well as the date you accessed the programme.

Citation order:

- Title of programme (in italics)
- Year of original transmission (in round brackets)
- Name of channel

- Day and month of original transmission
- Available at: URL
- Accessed: date

Example

In-text citation:

Technology offers the means to improve human ability (*Redesigning the human body*, 2006) …

Reference list:

Redesigning the human body (2006) BBC Radio 4, 25 September. Available at: http://www.bbc.co.uk/radio4/redesigninghumanbody/ (Accessed: 15 June 2008).

20.2 Television

20.2a Television programmes

Citation order:

- Title of programme (in italics)
- Year of transmission (in round brackets)
- Name of channel
- Date of transmission (day/month)

Example

In-text citation:

Vicky Pollard (*Little Britain*, 2005) exemplifies the temperamental teenager.

Reference list:

Little Britain (2005) BBC 2 Television, 23 June.

To quote something a character has said:

Example

In-text citation:

"yeah but no but …" (Pollard, 2005)

Reference list:

Pollard, V. (2005) *Little Britain*. BBC2 Television, 23 June.

20.2b Episodes of a television series

Citation order:

- Title of episode (in single quotation marks)
- Year of transmission (in round brackets)
- Title of programme (in italics)
- Series and episode numbers
- Name of channel
- Date of transmission (day/month)

Example

In-text citation:

Being dead gave Owen new opportunities to help the team ('A Day in the Death', 2008).

Reference list:

'A Day in the Death' (2008) *Torchwood*, Series 2, episode 10. BBC2 Television, 5 March.

20.2c Television programmes/series on DVDs

Citation order:

- Title of episode (in single quotation marks)
- Year of distribution (in round brackets)
- Title of programme/series (in italics)
- Series and episode numbers (if known)
- Director and writer
- Date of original broadcast (if known)
- [DVD]
- Place of distribution: Distribution company

Example

In-text citation:

The origins of the Doctor's most fearsome foe were revealed in 'Genesis of the Daleks' (2006).

Reference list:

'Genesis of the Daleks' (2006) *Doctor Who,* episode 1. Directed by David Maloney. Written by Terry Nation. First broadcast 1975 [DVD]. London: BBC DVD.

20.2d Separate episodes from DVD box-sets

Citation order:

- Title of episode (in single quotation marks)
- Year of distribution (in round brackets)
- Title of programme/series (in italics)
- In
- Title of compilation or box-set (in italics)
- [DVD]
- Place of distribution: Distributor

Example

In-text citation:

Close attention was paid to period details, for example the costumes of the dancers ('Episode 4', 2006).

Reference list:

'Episode 4' (2006) *The Mallen streak*. In *Catherine Cookson complete collection* [DVD]. London: ITV.

20.2e Television programmes viewed on the Internet

Citation order:

- Title of episode (in single quotation marks) if known; if not, use title of programme
- Year of transmission (in round brackets)
- Title of programme/series (in italics)
- Series and episode numbers (if known)
- Name of channel
- Day/month of transmission
- [Online]
- Available at: URL
- (Accessed: date)

Example

In-text citation:

The effects of the accident were portrayed graphically ('Love you', 2008).

Reference list:

'Love you' (2008) *Holby City*, Series 10, episode 4, BBC1 Television, 9 June. [Online] Available at: http://www.bbc.co.uk/iplayer/ (Accessed: 15 June 2008).

20.3 Audio/video downloads

Reference where you obtained music or video downloads, e.g. *iTunes.*

Citation order:

- Artist (if available; if not use title first)
- Year of distribution (in round brackets)
- Title of recording (in italics)
- Name of download site (in italics)
- [Download]
- Available at: URL
- Accessed: date

Example

In-text citation:

Mr Brightside was a major success (The Killers, 2004).

Reference list:

The Killers (2004) *Mr Brightside. iTunes* [Download]. Available at: http://www.apple.com/uk/itunes/ (Accessed: 13 November 2007).

20.4 Music or spoken word recordings on audio CDs/audio CD-ROMs

Citation order:

- Artist
- Year of distribution (in round brackets)
- Title of recording (in italics)
- [CD]
- Place of distribution: Distribution company

Example

In-text citation:

The band's finest album *(What's the story) Morning glory* (1995) …

Reference list:

Oasis (1995) *(What's the story) Morning glory* [CD]. London: Creation Records.

20.5 Music or spoken word recordings on audio cassettes

Citation order:

- Artist (if available; if not use title first)
- Year of distribution (in round brackets)
- Title of recording (in italics)
- [Audio cassette]
- Place of publication: Publisher

Example

In-text citation:

Determination is a key attribute (*It's your choice: selection skills for managers*, 1993).

Reference list:

It's your choice: selection skills for managers (1993) [Audio cassette]. London: Video Arts.

20.6 Liner notes

The liner notes in CD, DVD, vinyl and cassette containers often have information that can be referenced.

Citation order:

* Author
* Year (in round brackets)
* Title of liner notes text (in single quotation marks)
* In
* Title of recording (in italics)
* [CD liner notes]
* Place of distribution: Distribution company

Example

In-text citation:

Lennon and McCartney (1966) expressed the frustration of every new author:

"Dear Sir or Madam will you read my book?
It took me years to write, will you take a look?"

Reference list:

Lennon, J. and McCartney, P. (1966) *Paperback writer*. Liverpool: Northern Songs Ltd.

Example

In-text citation:

Thrills (1997, p.11) described Weller's lyrics as "sheer poetry".

Reference list:

Thrills, A. (1997) 'What a catalyst he turned out to be'. In *The very best of The Jam*. [CD liner notes]. London: Polydor.

20.7 Lyrics from a song

Include details of where you read the lyrics, such as a book, CD liner notes or web page.

Citation order:

* Lyricist
* Year of distribution (in round brackets)
* Title of song (in italics)
* Place of distribution: Distribution company

20.8 Musical scores

Citation order:

* Composer
* Year of publication (in round brackets)
* Title of score (in italics)
* Notes
* Place of publication: Publisher

Example

In-text citation:

The composer's haunting evocation of the sea in *Fingal's Cave* (Mendelssohn, 1999) …

Reference list:

Mendelssohn, F. (1999) *Fingal's Cave*. Edited from composer's notes by John Wilson. London: Initial Music Publishing.

20.9 Films/movies

20.9a Films/movies

Citation order:

- Title of film (in italics)
- Year of distribution (in round brackets)
- Director
- [Film]
- Place of distribution: Distribution company

Example

In-text citation:

Movies have been used to attack the President's policies (*Fahrenheit 9/11*, 2004).

Reference list:

Fahrenheit 9/11 (2004) Directed by Michael Moore [Film]. Santa Monica, California: Lions Gate Films.

20.9b Films on DVDs

Citation order:

- Title of film (in italics)
- Year of distribution (in round brackets)
- Directed by
- [DVD]
- Place of distribution: Distribution company.

Example

In-text citation:

Special effects can dominate a film, e.g. *The Matrix reloaded* (2003).

Reference list:

The Matrix reloaded (2003) Directed by A. & L. Wachowski [DVD]. Los Angeles: Warner Brothers Inc.

Many films on DVD come with additional material on other disks, such as interviews with actors and directors and out-takes. Here are examples for referencing some of this material:

20.9c Directors' commentaries on DVDs

Citation order:

- Name of commentator
- Year (in round brackets)
- Director's commentary (in single quotation marks)
- Name of film (in italics)
- Directed by ...
- [DVD]
- Place of distribution: Distribution company

Example

In-text citation:

The director thought this was a profitable franchise (Wachowski, 2003).

Reference list:

Wachowski, A. (2003) 'Director's commentary', *The Matrix reloaded*. Directed by A. & L. Wachowski [DVD]. Los Angeles: Warner Brothers Inc.

20.9d Interviews with directors of films

Citation order:

- Name of person interviewed
- Year of interview (in round brackets)
- Title of the interview (if any) (in single quotation marks)
- Interviewed with/Interviewed by
- Interviewer's name
- Title of film (in italics)
- [DVD]
- Place of distribution: Distribution company

Example

In-text citation:

When the story finally made it to the silver screen (*The Lord of the Rings: the two towers*, 2003) …

Reference list:

The Lord of the Rings: the two towers (2003) Directed by Peter Jackson [Video cassette]. New York: New Line Productions Inc.

Example

In-text citation:

The director thought this was a profitable franchise (Wachowski, 2003).

Reference list:

Wachowski, A. (2003) 'Interview with A. Wachowski'. Interviewed by L. Jones. *The Matrix reloaded* [DVD]. Los Angeles: Warner Brothers Inc.

20.9f Films on *Youtube*

Citation order:

- Name of person posting video
- Year video posted (in round brackets)
- Title of film or programme (in italics)
- Available at: URL
- (Accessed: date)

20.9e Films on video cassettes

Citation order:

- Title of film or programme (in italics)
- Year of distribution (in round brackets)
- Directed by
- [Video cassette]
- Place of distribution: Distribution company

Example

In-text citation:

Some made light of the discomfort (Raok2008, 2008) …

Reference list:

Raok2008 (2008) *For a cooler Tube*. Available at: http://www.youtube.com/watch?v=jXE6G9CYcJs (Accessed: 13 June 2008).

Example: with author/presenter

In-text citation:

Ben (2005) warned students to evaluate their sources.

Reference list:

Ben (2005) 'Critical thinking and the Internet', *BBC schools podcast* [Podcast]. 23 June. Available at: http://search.bbc.co.uk/cgi-bin/search/results.pl?tab=av&q=school%20podcast&recipe=all&scope=all&edition=(Accessed: 25 June 2005).

20.10 Podcasts

Although podcasts can be downloaded onto portable devices you should reference where it was published or displayed for download rather than trying to give "my iPod" as a source.

Citation order:

- Author/presenter

- Year that the site was published/last updated (in round brackets)

- Title of podcast (in single quotation marks)

- Title of Internet site (in italics)

- [Podcast]

- Day/month of posted message

- Available at: URL

- (Accessed: date)

Example: without author

In-text citation:

Internal networks are critical ('Structure', 2008) …

Reference list:

'Structure' (2008) *Oracle business sense with Guardian Unlimited* [Podcast]. 12 June. Available at: http://www.guardian.co.uk/podcast/0,,329509709,00.xml (Accessed: 27 June 2008).

20.11 Phonecasts

These are audio or video programmes transmitted to a user's mobile phone. The user dials a number to access the programme. Alternatively phonecasters can broadcast by using their telephones in place of microphones. Although phone calls are personal communications, it is possible to reference phonecasts if the access details are available in a publication or web page.

Harvard referencing style

Citation order:

- Title of phonecast (in single quotation marks)
- Year of production (in round brackets)
- Title of web page (in italics)
- Available at: URL
- (Accessed: date)

Example

In-text citation:

Zuckerberg created *Facebook* in 2004 ('A conversation with Mark Zuckerberg', 2007).

Reference list:

'A conversation with Mark Zuckerberg' (2007) *Phonecasting*. Available at: http://www.phonecasting.com/Channel/ViewChannel.aspx?id=1904 (Accessed: 1 July 2008).

20.12 Screencasts

Also called video screen captures, these are digital recordings of computer screen activity. Screencast videos can provide instructions for using software applications.

Citation order:

- Title of screencast (in single quotation marks)
- Year of production (in round brackets)
- Title of web page (in italics)
- [Screencast]
- Available at: URL
- (Accessed: date)

Example:

In-text citation:

An online video demonstrated functions ('Putting *Flickr* on *rails*', 2008).

Reference list:

'Putting *Flickr* on *rails*' (2008) *Show, don't tell* [Screencast]. Available at: http://www.rubyonrails.org/screencasts (Accessed: 27 June 2008).

20.13 Vidcasts/vodcasts

Video podcasts can be viewed on the Internet or downloaded for later viewing. So that readers can locate the original, cite and reference where you obtained the vidcast.

Citation order:

- Author
- Year that the site was published/last updated (in round brackets)
- Title of vidcast (in single quotation marks)
- Title of Internet site (in italics)
- Available at: URL
- (Accessed: date)

Example

In-text citation:

The vidcast was most informative (Walker and Carruthers, 2008).

Reference list:

Walker, A. and Carruthers, S. (2008) 'Episode 126: Storage on your network', *Lab rats!* Available at: http://www.labrats.tv/episodes/ep126.html (Accessed: 19 June 2008).

20.14 Microform (microfiche and microfilm)

Citation order:

* Author
* Year of publication (in round brackets)
* Title of microform (in italics)
* [Medium]
* Place of publication: Publisher

Example

In-text citation:

Data from Fritsch (1987) …

Reference list:

Fritsch, F.E. (1987) *The Fritsch collection: algae illustrations on microfiche* [Microfiche]. Ambleside: Freshwater Biological Association.

21. Interviews

Citation order:

* Name of person interviewed
* Year of interview (in round brackets)
* Title of the interview (if any) (in single quotation marks)
* Interview with/Interviewed by
* Interviewer's name
* Title of publication or broadcast (in italics)
* Day and month of interview

If published on the Internet add:

* [Online]
* Available at: URL
* (Accessed: date)

Example: newspaper interview

In-text citation:

Riley (2008) believed that "imagination has to be captured by reality".

Reference list:

Riley, B. (2008) 'The life of Riley'. Interview with Bridget Riley. Interviewed by Jonathan Jones for *The Guardian*, 5 July, p.33.

Example: television interview

In-text citation:

The Prime Minister avoided the question (Blair, 2003).

Reference list:

Blair, A. (2003) Interviewed by Jeremy Paxman for *Newsnight*, BBC2 Television, 2 February.

Example: Internet interview

In-text citation:

The Democrat appeared confident in the discussion (Obama, 2008).

Reference list:

Obama, B. (2008) Interviewed by Terry Moran for *ABC News*, 19 March. [Online] Available at: http://abcnews.go.com/Nightline/Vote2008/Story?id=4480133 (Accessed: 16 June 2008).

22. Public communications

Lectures, seminars, webinars, videoconferences/electronic discussion groups and bulletin boards/press releases, announcements/leaflets, advertisements/display boards/minutes of meetings/RSS feeds.

22.1 Lectures/seminars/webinars/videoconferences

Citation order:

- Author/speaker
- Year (in round brackets)
- Title of communication (in italics)
- [Medium]
- Day/Month

> **Example**
>
> **In-text citation:**
>
> Points of interest from the lecture (Brown, 2008) ...
>
> **Reference list:**
>
> Brown,T. (2008) *Contemporary furniture.* [Lecture to BSc Design Year 4]. 21 April.

22.2 Electronic discussion groups and bulletin boards

For personal e-mail correspondence see **23. Personal communications**. The following examples deal with e-mail correspondence made public in electronic conferences, discussion groups and bulletin boards.

Citation order:

- Author of message
- Year of message (in round brackets)
- Subject of the message (in single quotation marks)
- Discussion group or bulletin board (in italics)
- Date posted: day/month
- [Online]
- Available e-mail: e-mail address

> **Example**
>
> **In-text citation:**
>
> Debt cancellation was discussed by Peters (2008) ...
>
> **Reference list:**
>
> Peters, W.R. (2008) 'International finance questions', *British Business School Librarians Group discussion list*, 11 August [Online]. Available e-mail: lis-business@jiscmail.com

22.3 Entire discussion groups or bulletin boards

Citation order:

- Listname (in italics)
- Year of last update (in round brackets)
- [Online]
- Available e-mail: e-mail address
- (Accessed: date)

Example

In-text citation:

The *Photography news list* (2008) contains ...

Reference list:

Photography news list (2008) [Online]. Available e-mail: pnl@btinfonet. (Accessed: 3 April 2008).

22.4 Press releases/announcements

Citation order:

- Author/organisation
- Year issued (in round brackets)
- Title of communication (in italics)
- [Press release]
- Day/Month

If available online add:

- Available at: URL
- (Accessed: date)

Example

In-text citation:

Google Inc. (2008) offered ...

Reference list:

Google Inc. (2008) *Cartography for the masses* [Press release]. 24 June. Available at: http://www.google.com/intl/en/press/annc/ mapmaker_20080624.html (Accessed: 3 July 2008).

22.5 Leaflets

By their nature leaflets are unlikely to have all of the citation/reference elements, so include as much information as possible. It may also be useful to include a copy of a leaflet in an appendix to your assignment.

Citation order:

- Author (individual or corporate)
- Date (if available)
- Title (in italics)
- [Leaflet obtained ...]
- Date

Example

In-text citation:

Lloyds TSB Bank plc (no date) provides insurance for its mortgages.

Reference list:

Lloyds TSB Bank plc (no date) *Mortgages*. [Leaflet obtained in Newcastle branch], 4 June 2008.

22.6 Advertisements

If referencing information in an advertisement you will need to specify where it was seen. This might be online, in a newspaper, on television or in a location. Advertisements are often short-lived, so it is important to include the date you viewed them.

Citation order:

Cite and reference according to the medium in which the advertisement appeared; see examples overleaf.

Examples

In-text citation:

Recent advertisements by British Telecom (2008), Lloyds TSB (2008) and Northern Electric (2008) and that for the WOMAD festival (2007) ...

Reference list:
Example: television advertisement

British Telecom (2008) *Office relocation gremlins* [Advertisement on ITV1 Television]. 23 June.

Example: newspaper advertisement

The Guardian (2007), 'WOMAD festival' [Advertisement] 14 April, p.12.

Example: Internet advertisement

Lloyds TSB Bank plc (2008) *Selling your house?* [Advertisement] Available at http://www.hotmail.com (Accessed: 13 February 2008).

Example: billboard advertisement

Northern Electric plc (2008) *Green energy* [Billboard at Ellison Road, Dunston-on-Tyne]. 14 June.

22.7 Display boards (e.g. in museums)

It is very rare for an author to be given for information on display boards, so the example below uses the title first.

Citation order:

- Title (in italics)
- Year of production (if available)
- Display board at
- Name of venue, city
- Date observed

Example

In-text citation:

Martin's vivid colours are a noted feature of his work (*Paintings of John Martin*, 2008).

Reference list:

Paintings of John Martin (2008) Display board at Laing Art Gallery exhibition, Newcastle upon Tyne, 23 April 2008.

22.8 Minutes of meetings

Citation order

- Author (individual or group if identified)
- Year of meeting (in round brackets)
- Item being referenced (in single quotation marks)
- Title and date of meeting (in italics)
- Organisation
- Location of meeting

Example: with author identified

In-text citation:

Jones (2008) suggested work shadowing and mentoring.

Reference list:

Jones, T. (2008) 'Item 3.1: Developing our staff', *Minutes of staff development committee meeting 23 June 2008*, Western Health Trust, Shrewsbury.

Example: with group name

In-text citation:

The Staff development committee (2008) suggested work shadowing and mentoring.

Reference list:

Staff development committee (2008) 'Item 3.1: Developing our staff'. *Minutes of staff development committee meeting 23 June 2008*, Western Health Trust, Shrewsbury.

Examples

In-text citation:

This was disputed by Walters (2008).

Reference list:

Walters, F. (2008) Conversation with John Stephens, 13 August.

Walters, F. (2007) Letter to John Stephens, 23 January.

Walters, F. (2008) E-mail to John Stephens, 14 August.

Walters, F. (2007) Telephone conversation with John Stephens, 25 December.

Walters, F. (2008) Text message to John Stephens, 14 June.

Walters, F. (2007) Fax to John Stephens, 17 December.

22.9 RSS feeds

Really Simple Syndication is a method of notifying subscribers if a favourite web page, for example a news source, has been updated. You should reference the details of the original source, e.g. news web page or newly published journal article, not the RSS feed.

Note that both the in-text citations and references begin with the name of the sender of the communication. **NB:** You may need to seek permission from other parties in the correspondence before quoting them in your work. You might also include a copy of written communications in the appendix.

23. Personal communications

(see also **20.11 Phonecasts**)

Personal communications by face-to-face or telephone conversation, letter, e-mail, text message or fax can be referenced using:

Citation order:

- Sender/speaker/author
- Year of communication (in round brackets)
- Medium of communication
- Receiver of communication
- Day/month of communication

24. Genealogical sources

For the Harvard (author-date) referencing style, use the name of the person(s) and the date of the event as the in-text citation and provide the full details in the reference list.

24.1 Birth, marriage or death certificates

Citation order:

- Name of person (in single quotation marks)
- Year of event (in round brackets)
- Certified copy of ... certificate for (in italics)
- Full name of person (forenames, surname) (in italics)
- Day/month/year of event (in italics)
- Application number from certificate
- Location of Register Office

If you retrieved the certificate online, after application number from certificate add:

- Name of website (in italics)
- Year of last update (in round brackets)
- Available at: URL
- (Accessed: date)

> **Example**
>
> **In-text citation:**
>
> Amy was born in Bristol ('Amy Jane Bennett', 1874) ...
>
> **Reference list:**
>
> 'Amy Jane Bennett' (1874) *Certified copy of birth certificate for Amy Jane Bennett, 10 April 1874.* Application number 4001788/C. Bristol Register Office, Bristol, Gloucestershire, England.

24.2 Censuses

Citation order:

- Name of person (in single quotation marks)
- Year of census (in round brackets)
- Census return for... (in italics)
- Street, place, county (in italics)
- Registration sub-district (in italics)
- Public Record Office
- Piece number, folio number, page number

If you retrieved the certificate online, add

- Name of website (in italics)
- Year of last update (in round brackets)
- Available at: URL
- (Accessed: date)

> **Example**
>
> **In-text citation:**
>
> Thomas Wilson moved to Willington in the 1850s ('Thomas Wilson', 1861).
>
> **Reference list:**
>
> 'Thomas Wilson' (1861) *Census return for New Row, Willington, St Oswald sub-district, County Durham.* Public Record Office: PRO RG9/3739, folio 74, p.11. *Ancestry* (2008). Available at: http://www.ancestry.co.uk (Accessed: 3 July 2008).

24.3 Parish registers

Citation order:

- Name of person (in single quotation marks)
- Year of event (in round brackets)
- Baptism, marriage or burial of
- Full name of person (forenames, surname)
- Day/month/year of event
- Title of register (in italics)

If you retrieved the certificate online, add

- Name of website (in italics)
- Year of last update (in round brackets)
- Available at: URL
- (Accessed: date)

Example

In-text citation:

Mary and Edward's wedding ('Edward Robson and Mary Slack', 1784) …

Reference list:

'Edward Robson and Mary Slack' (1784) Marriage of Edward Robson and Mary Slack, 6 May 1784. *St Augustine's Church Alston, Cumberland marriage register 1784-1812. Genuki.* (2004) Available at: http://www.genuki.org.uk/big/eng/CUL/Alston/MALS1701.html (Accessed: 3 July 2008).

24.4 Military records

Citation order:

- Name of person (in single quotation marks)
- Year of publication (in round brackets)
- Title of publication (in italics)
- Publication details

If you retrieved the document online

- Available at: URL
- (Accessed: date)

Example

In-text citation:

Private Wakenshaw fought on even after losing his arm ('Adam Herbert Wakenshaw VC', 2008).

Reference list:

'Adam Herbert Wakenshaw VC' (2008) *Commonwealth War Graves Commission casualty details.* Available at: http://www.cwgc.org/search/casualty_details.aspx?casualty=2212745 (Accessed: 2 July 2008).

---

25. Manuscripts

If the author of a manuscript is known:

Citation order:

- Author
- Year (in round brackets)
- Title of manuscript (in italics)
- Date (if available)
- Name of collection containing manuscript and reference number
- Location of manuscript in archive or repository

Harvard referencing style

Example

In-text citation:

The architect enjoyed a close relationship with his patron (Newton, 1785).

Reference list:

Newton,W. (1785) *Letter to William Ord, 23 June*. Ord Manuscripts 324 E11/4, Northumberland Collections Service, Woodhorn.

Example

In-text citation:

Consulting the family records (British Library, Lansdowne MS) the author discovered …

Reference list:

British Library, Lansdowne MS.

Note that no date is given for a collection in the text or in the reference list as the collection contains items of various dates.

Where the author of a manuscript is not known:

Citation order:

- Title of manuscript (in italics)
- Year (if known, in round brackets)
- Name of collection containing manuscript, and reference number
- Location of manuscript in archive or repository

Example

In-text citation:

Expenditure was high in this period (*Fenham journal*, 1795).

Reference list:

Fenham journal (1795) Ord Manuscripts, 324 E12, Northumberland Collections Service, Woodhorn .

To refer to a whole collection of manuscripts (MS), use the name of the collection:

Citation order:

- Location of collection in archive or repository
- Name of collection

Section E: Alternatives to the Harvard (author-date) style

This section has examples of some alternatives to the Harvard referencing style that are used by some university departments and publishers. These are OSCOLA (used in many Law departments), the American Psychological Association (APA), the Modern Language Association (MLA) and the Modern Humanities Research Association (MHRA) referencing styles. Examples of the most commonly used sources are given for each style, along with sample passages of text to illustrate citations, and examples of reference lists using these styles. For advice on how to reference other sources, check the Harvard examples and re-arrange the elements of the reference listed there to match the requirements of these alternative styles.
Remember to apply the referencing style you are using consistently throughout your work.

E1: Oxford Standard for the Citation Of Legal Authorities (OSCOLA)

As noted in previous editions of *Cite them right*, there are established guidelines for the referencing of legal materials which vary from the procedures in the rest of this book. Many UK law schools and legal publications use the Oxford Standard for Citation of Legal Authorities (OSCOLA); examples of referencing common legal sources in the OSCOLA format are given below. For more information see Meredith, S. and Endicott, T. (2006) *Oxford Standard for Citation of Legal Authorities*. Available at: http://denning.law.ox.ac.uk/published /oscola_2006.pdf (Accessed: 30 June 2008).

Conventions in OSCOLA referencing style

- OSCOLA uses numeric references in the text linked to full citations in footnotes
- There are no in-text citations
- Very little punctuation is used
- Well-established abbreviations are used for legal sources such as law reports and Parliamentary publications
- OSCOLA assumes that you are referencing UK legal sources. If you are writing about legal material in several countries, use abbreviations of the nations to denote different jurisdictions, e.g. Access to Justice Act 1999 (UK); Homeland Security Act 2001 (USA).

How to reference sources in the OSCOLA style

E1.1 Books

Citation order:

- Author,
- Book title (in italics)
- (Publisher, Place Date)

> **Example**
>
> **Reference list:**
>
> C.M.V. Clarkson, *Criminal law: text and materials* (Sweet & Maxwell, London 2007).

E1.2 Journal articles

Citation order:

- Author,
- Article title (in single quotation marks)
- (Year)
- Volume number
- Abbreviated journal title,
- First page number

Example

Reference list:

A.J. Roberts, 'Evidence: bad character - pre-Criminal Justice Act 2003 law' (2008) 4 Crim L R, 303.

E1.3 e-journal articles

Note: OSCOLA (Meredith and Endicott, 2006, p.20) suggests that for print articles the year is enclosed in round brackets, but for e-journal articles that the year is enclosed in square brackets.

Citation order:

* Author
* 'Article title' (in single quotation marks)
* [Year]
* Volume number
* Abbreviated journal title,
* First page number
* <URL>
* accessed date

Example

Reference list:

C. Behan and I. O'Donnell 'Prisoners, politics and the polls: enfranchisement and the burden of responsibility' [2008] 48(3) Brit J Criminol, 31 <doi:10.1093/bjc/azn004> accessed 6 July 2008.

E1.4 Bills (either House of Commons or House of Lords)

Citation order:

* Short title
* House in which it originated
* Parliamentary session (in round brackets)
* Bill number (in square brackets for Commons bills, no brackets for Lords bills)

Example

Reference list:

Transport HC Bill (1999-2000) [8]

Transport HL Bill (2007-08) 1.

E1.5 UK Statutes (Acts of Parliament)

A major change in the citation of UK legal sources took place in 1963. Before this, an Act was cited according to the regnal year (i.e. the number of years since the monarch's accession).

E1.5a Pre-1963 statutes

Citation order:

* Title of Act and Year
* Regnal year
* Name of sovereign
* Chapter number

Example

Reference list:

Act of Supremacy 1534 (26 Hen 8 c1)

E1.5b Post-1963 statutes

Use the short title of an Act, with the year in which it was enacted.

Citation order:

- Short title of Act
- Year enacted

Example

Reference list:

Access to Justice Act 1999.

E1.5c Parts of Acts

Citation order:

- Short title of Act
- Year enacted
- Pt for Part
- s for section number
- Sub-section number (in round brackets)
- Paragraph number (in round brackets)

Example

Reference list:

Finance Act 2007, Pt1, s 2(1)(b).

E1.6 Statutory Instruments

Citation order:

- Name/title
- SI Year/number

Example

Reference list:

Terrorism (United Nations Measures) Order 2001 SI 2001/3365.

E1.7 Command Papers

Citation order:

- Author
- Title (in single quotation marks)
- Paper number and year (in round brackets)

Example

Reference list:

Lord Chancellor's Department, 'Government policy on archives'. (Cm 4516, 1999).

E1.8 Law reports (cases)

Citation order:

- Case (in italics)
- Date, volume number and abbreviation for name of report and first page of report

---

Examples

Reference list:

Hazell v Hammersmith and Fulham London Borough Council [1992] 2 AC 1

(Date in square brackets - in accordance with the convention used for legal material)

OSCOLA referencing style

R v Edwards (John) (1991) 93 Cr App R 48

(Date in round brackets because there is also a volume number).

E1.9 Hansard

Hansard is the official record of debates and speeches given in Parliament. Note that OSCOLA (2006) suggests a form of referencing for Hansard that varies from that given by the House of Commons Information Office (2008) *Factsheet G17: The Official Report*. After discussion with the author of OSCOLA, we suggest that you use the form given in *Factsheet G17: The Official Report*.

Citation order

- Abbreviation of House
- Deb (for Debates)
- Date of debate
- Volume number
- Column number

Examples

Reference list:

HC Deb 19 June 2008 vol 477 c1183

• If you are citing a Commons Written Answer, use the suffix W after the column number:

e.g. HC Deb 19 June 2008 vol 477 c1106W

• If you are citing a Lords Written Answer, use the prefix WA before the column number:

e.g. HL Deb 19 June 2008 vol 702 cWA200

• Use the suffix WS if you are citing a Written Statement:

e.g. HC Deb 13 November 2001 c134WS

• Use the suffix WH if you are citing a debate in Westminster Hall:

e.g. HC Deb 21 May 2008 vol 476 c101WH

• If quoting very old Hansards it is usual, although optional, to include the series number:

Hansard HC (5th series) vol. 878 c69 (13 January 1907)

• In 2006 the earlier system of Standing Committees was replaced by Public Bill Committees.

Standing Committee Hansard should be cited as follows:

SC Deb (A) 13 May 1998 c345.

The new Public Bill Committees would be cited thus:

Health Bill Deb 30 January 2007 c12-15

unless the Bill title is so long that this becomes ridiculous. In this case use:

PBC Deb (Bill 99) 30 January 2007 c12-15

or, where the context makes the Bill obvious,

PBC Deb 30 January 2007 c12-15

• In Hansard itself, citations are given in the form [Official Report, 17 December 1979; Vol. 976, c. 37].

For more information on the use of Hansard, see *Factsheet G17: The Official Report* (2008) produced by the House of Commons Information Office. Available at: http://www.parliament.uk/documents/upload/g17.pdf (Accessed: 2 July 2008).

A fully searchable version of Hansard from 1988 for the Commons and from 1995 for the Lords is available online at http://www.publications.parliament.uk/pa/pahansard.htm (Accessed: 2 July 2008).

Example

Reference list:

Tuberculosis (Scotland) Order 2005 (S.S.I. 2005/434).

E1.10 Legislation from devolved Assemblies

OSCOLA (2006) does not give examples of devolved Assembly legislation. Based on Great Britain. Ministry of Justice (2008) *How we cite legislation*. Available at: http://www.statutelaw.gov.uk/help/How_we_cite_legislation.htm (Accessed: 7 July 2008), we suggest the following forms:

E1.10a Acts of the Scottish Parliament

For Acts of the post-devolution Scottish Parliament, replace the Chapter number with "asp" (meaning Act of the Scottish Parliament).

Citation order:

- Title of Act including year
- asp number.

Example

Reference list:

Budget (Scotland) Act 2004 asp 2.

E1.10b Scottish Statutory Instruments

Citation order:

- Title includes year
- Scottish Statutory Instrument (S.S.I.) number (in round brackets)

E1.10c Acts of the Northern Ireland Assembly

Citation order:

- Title of Act (Northern Ireland)
- Year
- Chapter number

Example

Reference list:

Ground Rents Act (Northern Ireland) 2001 c.5

E1.10d Statutory Rules of Northern Ireland

The Northern Ireland Assembly may pass Statutory Instruments. These are called Statutory Rules of Northern Ireland.

Citation order:

- Title of Rule (Northern Ireland)
- Year
- (Year/SR number)

Example

Reference list:

Smoke Flavourings Regulations (Northern Ireland) 2005 (SR 2005/76).

OSCOLA referencing style

E1.10e Welsh Assembly legislation

The Welsh Assembly may pass Assembly Measures, which are primary legislation but are subordinate to UK statutes. At the date of writing (6 August 2008) no Assembly Measures had been passed. The Welsh Assembly may pass Statutory Instruments. As well as the SI number and year, Welsh Statutory Instruments have a W. number.

Citation order:

- Title of order (Wales)
- Year
- Year/SI number (W. number)

Example

Reference list:

The Bluetongue (Wales) Order 2003 Welsh Statutory Instrument 2003/326 (W.47).

E1.11 European Union legislation

EU legislation may be directives, decisions and regulations.

Citation order:

- Legislation type
- (EC)
- Number and title
- Publication detail from the Official Journal (OJ) of the European Communities

Example

Reference list:

Council Directive (EC) 2008/52 on certain aspects of mediation in civil and commercial matters [2008] OJ L136/3.

E1.12 United States legal material

For information on citing and referencing US legal material see *The Bluebook: a uniform system of citation* (2005) Harvard Law Review Association. A useful online guide is Martin, P.W. (2007) *Introduction to basic legal citation*. Available at: http://www.law.cornell.edu/citation/ (Accessed: 6 July 2008).

OSCOLA sample text

The Judge noted the case of *R. v. Edwards*.[1] The Access to Justice Act 1999[2] and the Terrorism (United Nations Measures) Order[3] strengthened this interpretation. An alternative view was suggested by Clarkson[4] and most recently by Behan and O'Donnell.[5]

OSCOLA sample reference list

1. *R v Edwards (John)* (1991) 93 Cr App R 48
2. Access to Justice Act 1999.
3. Terrorism (United Nations Measures) Order 2001 SI 2001/3365.
4. C.M.V. Clarkson, *Criminal law: text and materials* (Sweet & Maxwell, London 2007).
5. C. Behan and I. O'Donnell 'Prisoners, politics and the polls: enfranchisement and the burden of responsibility' [2008] 48(3) Brit J Criminol, 31 <doi:10.1093/bjc/azn004> accessed 6 July 2008.

E2. American Psychological Association (APA) referencing style

The APA referencing style is used in some social science subjects. It uses an author-date format, like Harvard, to identify details in the text. Full details are given in an alphabetical list of references.

Conventions in APA referencing style

Multiple authors and et al.

- The APA insists that up to five authors are listed by name in an in-text citation:

Example

Smith, Jones, Cassidy, Grey and Anders (2006) …

- If there are six or more authors use the first author and et al. for the in-text citation:

Example

Games can assist recovery (Weathers et al., 1981) …

- But all authors should be listed in your reference list:

Example

Weathers, L., Bedell, J.R., Marlowe, H., Gordon, R.E., Adams, J., Reed, V., Palmer, J., & Gordon, K.K. (1981). Using psychotherapeutic games to train patients' skills. In R.E. Gordon and K.K. Gordon, (Eds.) *Systems of treatment for the mentally ill* (pp.109-124). New York: Grune and Stratton, 1981.

Titles

- The titles of sources are italicised, as are volume numbers of journal articles, but not issue or page numbers.

- Titles of articles within journals, or chapters within books, are not enclosed in quotation marks.

Page numbers

- Page numbers for book chapters are given immediately after the title of the book in round brackets and before publication details.

Internet sources

- Internet sources should be indicated by Retrieved month/day/year from URL:

Example

Upton health centre: surgery times. (2008). Retrieved June 14, 2008, from http://www.uptonnhs.org.uk.

Footnotes or endnotes

- You can use footnotes or endnotes in the APA referencing style to bring in additional information. Use a **superscript number** for the footnote (see **Glossary**).

How to reference common sources

E2.1 Books

Citation order:

- Author/editor
- Year of publication (in round brackets)
- Title (in italics)
- Edition (only include the edition number if it is not the first edition)
- Place of publication: Publisher

Example

In-text citation:

Earlier analysis (Freud, 1936, p.54) …

Reference list:

Freud, A. (1936). *The ego and the mechanisms of defense*. New York: International Universities Press.

E2.3 Journal articles

Citation order:

- Author (surname followed by initials)
- Year of publication (in round brackets)
- Title of article
- Title of journal (in italics)
- Volume number (in italics)
- Issue (in round brackets) and page numbers

E2.2 Chapters/sections of edited books

Citation order:

- Author of the chapter/section (surname followed by initials)
- Year of publication (in round brackets)
- Title of chapter/section
- In
- Name of editor of book (Ed.)
- Title of book (in italics)
- Page numbers of chapter/section (in round brackets)
- Place of publication: Publisher

Example

In-text citation:

Research by Frosch (2002) …

Reference list:

Frosch, A. (2002). Transference: Psychic reality and material reality. *Psychoanalytic Psychology, 19*(4):603-633.

E2.4 Journal articles (e-journals)

Citation order:

- Author
- Year of publication (in round brackets)
- Title of article
- Title of journal (in italics)
- Volume number (in italics)
- Issue (in round brackets) and page numbers
- Retrieved
- Date of access
- from Name of collection (in italics)
- URL of collection

Example

In-text citation:

The view proposed by Leites (1990, p.444) …

Reference list:

Leites, N. (1990). Transference interpretations only? In A.H. Esman (Ed.) *Essential papers on transference* (pp.434-454). New York: New York University Press.

Example

In-text citation:

Violence is a factor in many instances of transference (Shubs, 2008).

Reference list:

Shubs, C.H. (2008). Transference issues concerning victims of violent crime and other traumatic incidents of adulthood. *Psychoanalytic Psychology, 25*(1), 122-141. Retrieved June 14, 2008, from *Ovid* http://ovidsp.uk.ovid.com/spb/ovidweb.cgi

Example

In-text citation:

As suggested by one website (*Learn to profile people*, 2008) …

Reference list:

Learn to profile people. (2008). Retrieved June 14, 2008, from http://lifehacker.com/346372/learn-to-profile-people.

E2.5 Organisation or personal Internet sites

Citation order:

- Author
- Year that the site was published/last updated (in round brackets)
- Title of Internet site (in italics)
- Retrieved
- Date of access
- from URL

This sample text shows how sources would be cited:

The theory of transference was developed by the research of Leites (1990) and Frosch (2002). Shubs (2008) has recently identified violence as a factor in transference. There are many other factors in transference (Bisby, 2005).

The reference list for the above text would be:

Bisby, L.B. (1993). Transference. *Journal of Metapsychology*. Article 101. Retrieved June 14, 2008, from http://www.tir.org/metapsy/jom/101_transfer.html.

Frosch, A. (2002). Transference: Psychic reality and material reality. *Psychoanalytic Psychology, 19*(4):603-633.

Leites, N. (1990). Transference interpretations only? In A.H. Esman, (Ed.) *Essential papers on transference* (pp.434-454). New York: New York University Press.

Shubs, C.H. (2008). Transference issues concerning victims of violent crime and other traumatic incidents of adulthood. *Psychoanalytic Psychology, 25*(1), 122-141. Retrieved June 14, 2008, from *Ovid* http://ovidsp.uk.ovid.com/spb/ovidweb.cgi.

Example

In-text citation:

There are several career paths (British Psychological Association, 2008) …

Reference list:

British Psychological Association (2008) *Areas of psychology*. Retrieved June 15, 2008, from http://www.bps.org.uk/careers/areas/areas_home.cfm

For web pages where no author can be identified, you should use the web page's title. If no title either, use the URL.

APA referencing style

E3. Modern Language Association (MLA) referencing style

The MLA referencing style is sometimes used in humanities subjects, including languages and literature. Emphasis is placed on the author's name (or if not available, the title of the source). The authors' full names, as written on the title pages, should be used. Sources are listed in a **Cited Works List** at the end of your work. Sources that are not cited in your text can be included in **footnotes** or **endnotes** (see **Glossary**). In-text citations use the author's name and if possible a page number within the source. To find the full details of the source being cited, the reader must refer to the Cited Works List.

Conventions when using the MLA referencing style

Author's name

• For in-text references and footnotes, give the author's name as forename(s) followed by surname, e.g. Peter Leach. For the Cited Works List, give surname, then forename(s), e.g. Leach, Peter.

Titles

• The titles of sources are underlined and not italicised

• Capitalise the first word, all nouns, verbs and adjectives. Capitalise articles if they are the first words of a subtitle after a colon, e.g.

Cite Them Right: The Essential Referencing Guide

Pagination

• Do not use p. or pp.

Web addresses

• Web addresses should be indicated by angle brackets around the

URL, e.g. < URL >. Note that when using the MLA referencing style, the date that you accessed an online resource is placed before the URL.

Footnotes or endnotes

• You can use footnotes or endnotes (see **Glossary**) in the MLA referencing style to bring in additional information. Use a superscript number for the footnote (see **Glossary**).

How to cite common sources in your text

You can phrase your text to note the author's view:

> **Example**
>
> Francis Wheen compared Thatcher's dislike of trade unions to that of Victorian mill-owners (23).

Or you can cite the author and page number after the section of their work you have referred to:

> **Example**
>
> Margaret Thatcher had a "hostility to organised labour that would have won the respect of any grim-visaged Victorian mill-owner" (Wheen 23).

Note that there is no comma between the author and the page number and that there is no p. before the page number.

If there is no author, use the title of the source and the page number:

> **Example**
>
> The Percy tomb has been described as "one of the master-pieces of medieval European art" (Treasures of Britain 84).

The following sample piece of text shows how various sources would be included as in-text citations:

Worsley (<u>Classical Architecture</u>) highlighted the variety of styles that eighteenth century architects employed in their buildings. Initially British architects relied upon the designs of Andrea Palladio, a sixteenth century Italian architect, who was believed to have studied ancient Roman buildings (<u>Palladio's Italian Villas</u>). As the century progressed, however, more authentic Roman examples were studied, particularly after the discovery of Pompeii (Nappo). Rich patrons wanted designs in the latest fashion and among those to profit from this demand was Robert Adam, who published his studies of Roman buildings (Adam). With this first-hand knowledge he designed many country houses and public buildings. His work was not always as revolutionary as he claimed (Worsley 265), but it certainly impressed clients. Peter Leach noted that Adam was even able to take over projects begun by other architects, as at Kedleston in Derbyshire (159).

Although most patrons favoured classical styles, Horace Walpole suggested that the Gothic style was "our architecture", the national style of England (Walpole, cited in Lang 251). Alexandrina Buchanan suggested that Gothic style signified ancient lineage and the British Constitution (43).

How to reference common sources in the Cited Works List

E3.1 Books

Citation order:

- Author/editor (surname, forename)
- Title (underlined)
- Edition (only include the edition number if it is not the first edition)
- Place of publication: Publisher
- Year of publication

Example

Cited Works List:

Worsley, Giles. <u>Classical Architecture in Britain: The Heroic Age</u>. London: Published for the Paul Mellon Centre for Studies in British Art by Yale University Press, 1995.

E3.2 Chapters/sections of edited books

Citation order:

- Author of the chapter/section (surname, forename)
- Title of chapter/section (in double quotation marks)
- Title of book (underlined)
- Ed. and name of editor of book
- Place of publication: Publisher
- Year of publication
- Page numbers of chapter/section

MLA referencing style

> **Example**
>
> **Cited Works List:**
>
> Buchanan, Alexandrina. "Interpretations of Medieval Architecture." <u>Gothic Architecture and Its Meanings 1550-1830</u>. Ed. Michael Hall. Reading: Spire Books, 2002, 27-52.

E3.3 Journal articles

Citation order:

- Author (surname, forename)
- Title of article (in double quotation marks)
- Title of journal (underlined)
- Volume number and issue number
- Year of publication (in round brackets) followed by colon
- Page numbers of journal article

> **Example**
>
> **Cited Works List:**
>
> Leach, Peter. "James Paine's Design for the South Front of Kedleston Hall: Dating and Sources." <u>Architectural History</u> 40 (1997):159-70.

E3.4 Electronic journal articles (e-journals)

Citation order:

- Author (surname, forename or initial)
- Title of article (in double quotation marks)
- Title of journal (underlined)
- Volume and issue numbers
- Year (in round brackets) followed by colon

- Page numbers of article
- Name of collection (underlined)
- Date of access
- <URL of collection>

> **Example**
>
> **Cited Works List:**
>
> Lang, S. "The Principles of the Gothic Revival in England." <u>Journal of the Society of Architectural Historians</u> 25.4 (1966): 240-267. <u>JSTOR</u>. 3 June 2008. <http://www.jstor.org/stable/988353>.

E3.5 Organisation or personal Internet sites

Citation order:

- Author (surname, forename)
- Title of Internet site (underlined)
- Year that the site was published/last updated
- Date of access
- <URL>

> **Example**
>
> **Cited Works List:**
>
> Nappo, Salvatore. <u>Pompeii: Its Discovery and Preservation</u>. 2003. 2 June 2008. <http://www.bbc.co.uk/history/ancient/romans/pompeii_rediscovery_01.shtml>

For web pages where no author can be identified, you should use the web page's title. If no title either, use the URL.

Nappo, Salvatore. <u>Pompeii: Its Discovery and Preservation</u>. 2003. 2 June 2008. <http://www.bbc.co.uk/history/ancient/romans/pompeii_rediscovery_01.shtml>.

Example

Cited Works List:

<u>Palladio's Italian Villas</u>. 2005. 2 June 2008. <http://www.boglewood.com/palladio/>.

Palladio's Italian Villas. 2005. 2 June 2008. <http://www.boglewood.com/palladio/>.

Worsley, Giles. <u>Classical Architecture in Britain: The Heroic Age</u>. London: Published for the Paul Mellon Centre for Studies in British Art by Yale University Press, 1995.

Cited Works List

All sources are listed alphabetically in the Cited Works List, giving all details of author, title and publication. In keeping with the emphasis upon authors' names, the first line of the reference is not indented, but subsequent lines are, so that authors' names are easily identifiable. This is an example of a Cited Works List for the sample text on page 83:

For more information on using the MLA referencing style, see http://www.mla.org/

Adam, Robert. <u>Ruins of the Palace of the Emperor Diocletian at Spalatro in Dalmatia</u>. London,1764. <u>Eighteenth Century Collections Online</u>. 2 June 2008 <http://galenet.galegroup.com/servlet/ECCO>.

Buchanan, Alexandrina. "Interpretations of Medieval Architecture." <u>Gothic Architecture and Its Meanings 1550-1830</u>. Ed. Michael Hall. Reading: Spire Books, 2002, pp. 27-52.

Lang, S. "The Principles of the Gothic Revival in England." <u>Journal of the Society of Architectural Historians</u> 25.4 (1966): 240-267, <u>JSTOR</u>. 3 June 2008. <http://www.jstor.org/stable/988353>.

Leach, Peter. "James Paine's Design for the South Front of Kedleston Hall: Dating and Sources." <u>Architectural History</u> 40 (1997):159-70.

E4. Modern Humanities Research Association (MHRA) referencing style

Sections D and **E2** showed how to cite and reference sources using author-date referencing styles, using the author's name and the year of publication in your text. This section of *Cite them right* will provide details of a numeric referencing style published by the Modern Humanities Research Association. This is used in some arts and humanities publications.

Citing sources in your text

Instead of naming authors in the text, which can be distracting for the reader, numbers are used to denote citations. These numbers in the text are linked to a full reference in footnotes or endnotes and in your bibliography (see **Glossary**). Word processing software such as Microsoft Word can create this link between citation number and full reference.

Cited publications are numbered in the order in which they are first referred to in the text. They are usually identified by a **superscript number** (see **Glossary**), e.g. Thomas corrected this error.[1]

If the citation is not shown by a superscript number it might be in round brackets, e.g. Thomas corrected this error.(1)

Or it might be in square brackets, e.g. Thomas corrected this error.[1]

Conventions when using the MHRA referencing style

Footnotes and endnotes

- The use of modern word processing software has led to a resurgence in the use of footnotes or endnotes. These can be used in MHRA referencing style to keep bibliographic details out of the flow of text, and can also be used to add additional information that may not fit easily into the main body of your work. Check whether footnotes or endnotes are preferred for the work you are producing.

First citation and shortened subsequent citations

- Note that the first time you cite a source, you should give full details in the footnote or endnote. Subsequent entries to the same source can be abbreviated to author's surname and the first few words of the title, plus a page number if you are citing a specific part of the text, e.g.

  Worsley, *Classical Architecture*, p.25.

  The sample text on page 89 shows examples of a first citation and subsequent citation of this book by Worsley.

  Note that the use of shortened citations, which are more precise, replaces *op. cit.* (from Latin, *opere citato*, meaning "in the work cited"), as used in earlier publications and previous editions of *Cite them right*

- As well as footnotes or endnotes you should list all your sources, including those you have read but not cited, in a bibliography at the end of your work.

ibid.

- *ibid.* (from Latin, *ibidem* means "in the same place"). If two (or more) consecutive references are from the same source then the second (or others) is cited *ibid.*, e.g.

---

1. Gester, Paul., *Finding Information on the Internet*, (London: John Wiley, 1999), pp.133-181.

2. *ibid*., p.155.

3. *ibid*., p.170.

Capitalisation

- Capitilise the first letter of the first word, all nouns, verbs, and adjectives. Also capitalise articles if they are the first words of a subtitle after a colon, e.g. *Cite Them Right: The Essential Referencing Guide*.

Internet addresses (URLs)

- The Internet address is given in full, but with < in front and > after the address, e.g. <http://news.bbc.co.uk> then [accessed date].

Author names

- Note that in the footnotes author names should be forename followed by surname, e.g. Francis Wheen. In the bibliography, author names should be surname followed by forename, e.g. Wheen, Francis.

Commas

- Use commas to separate the elements of the reference.

How to reference common sources in your bibliography

E4.1 Books

Citation order:

- Author/editor
- Title (in italics)
- Edition (only include the edition number if it is not the first edition)
- Place of publication: Publisher, Year of publication (all in round brackets)

Example

Bibliography:

Worsley, Giles. *Classical Architecture in Britain: The Heroic Age*. (London: Published for the Paul Mellon Centre for Studies in British Art by Yale University Press, 1995).

E4.2 e-books

Citation order:

- Author/editor
- Title (in italics)
- Edition (only include the edition number if it is not the first edition)
- Place of publication: Publisher, Year of publication (all in round brackets)
- In
- Title of online collection (in italics)
- <URL of collection>
- [accessed date]

Example

Bibliography:

Adam, Robert, *Ruins of the Palace of the Emperor Diocletian at Spalatro in Dalmatia*, London, (1764). In *Eighteenth Century Collections Online*, <http://galenet.galegroup.com/servlet/ECCO> [accessed 2 June 2008].

MHRA referencing style

E4.3 Chapters/sections of edited books

Citation order:

- Author of the chapter/section
- Title of chapter/section (in single quotation marks)
- In
- Title of book (in italics)
- ed. by
- Name of editor of book
- Place of publication: Publisher, Year of publication (all in round brackets)
- Page numbers of chapter/section

Example

Bibliography:

Buchanan, Alexandrina, 'Interpretations of Medieval Architecture'. In *Gothic Architecture and Its Meanings 1550-1830*, ed. by Michael Hall (Reading: Spire Books, 2002), pp. 27-52.

E4.4 Journal articles

Citation order:

- Author
- Title of article (in single quotation marks)
- Title of journal (in italics and capitalise first letter of each word in title, except for linking words such as and, of, the, for)
- Volume and issue numbers
- Year of publication (in round brackets)
- Page numbers of article (not preceded by pp.)

Example

Bibliography:

Leach, Peter, 'James Paine's Design for the South Front of Kedleston Hall: Dating and Sources', *Architectural History*, 40 (1997),159-70.

E4.5 e-journal articles

Citation order:

- Author
- Title of article (in single quotation marks)
- Title of journal (in italics and capitalise first letter of each word in title, except for linking words such as and, of, the, for)
- Volume. Issue number
- Year of publication (in round brackets)
- Page numbers of article
- In
- Name of collection (in italics)
- <URL>
- [accessed date]

Example

Bibliography:

Lang, S., 'The Principles of the Gothic Revival in England', *Journal of the Society of Architectural Historians*, 25.4 (1966), 240-267. In *JSTOR*, <http://www.jstor.org/stable/988353> [accessed 3 June 2008].

MHRA referencing style

E4.6 Organisation or personal Internet sites

Citation order:

- Author
- Title of Internet site (in italics)
- Year that the site was published/last updated (in round brackets)
- <URL>
- [accessed date]

Example

Bibliography:

Nappo, Salvatore Ciro, *Pompeii: Its Discovery and Preservation*, (2003), <http://www.bbc.co.uk/history/ancient/romans/pompeii_rediscovery_01.shtml> [accessed 2 June 2008].

For web pages where no author can be identified, you should use the web page's title. If no title either, use the URL.

Example

Bibliography:

Palladio's Italian Villas (2005) <http://www.boglewood.com/palladio/> [accessed 2 June 2008].

E4.7 Manuscripts in archives

Citation order:

- Place
- Name of archive
- Reference number
- Description of document

Example

Bibliography:

London. The National Archives: Public Record Office PROB 3/42/93 Inventory of Elizabeth Bennett of Deptford, 10 November 1743.

This sample piece of text shows how various sources would be included as in-text citations:

Worsley's *Classical Architecture* highlighted the variety of styles that eighteenth century architects employed in their buildings.[1] Initially British architects relied upon the designs of Andrea Palladio, a sixteenth century Italian architect, who was believed to have studied ancient Roman buildings.[2] As the century progressed, however, more authentic Roman examples were studied, particularly after the discovery of Pompeii.[3] Rich patrons wanted designs in the latest fashion and among those to profit from this demand was Robert Adam, who published his studies of Roman buildings.[4] With this first-hand knowledge he designed many country houses and public buildings.[5] His work was not always as revolutionary as he claimed,[6] but it certainly impressed clients. Adam was even able to take over projects begun by other architects, as at Kedleston in Derbyshire.[7]

Although most patrons favoured classical styles, Horace Walpole suggested that the Gothic style was "our architecture", the national style of England.[8] Later authors have suggested that Gothic signified ancient lineage and the British Constitution.[9]

The footnotes for this piece of text would look like this:

1. Giles Worsley, *Classical Architecture in Britain: The Heroic Age*. (London: Published for the Paul Mellon Centre for Studies in British Art by Yale University Press, 1995).

2. *Palladio's Italian Villas*, (2005), <http://www.boglewood.com/ palladio/> [accessed 2 June 2008].

3. Salvatore Ciro Nappo, *Pompeii: Its Discovery and Preservation*, (2003), <http://www.bbc.co.uk/history/ancient/ romans/pompeii_rediscovery_ 01.shtml> [accessed 2 June 2008].

4. Robert Adam, *Ruins of the Palace of the Emperor Diocletian at Spalatro in Dalmatia*, London, (1764), in *Eighteenth Century Collections Online*, <http://galenet.galegroup.com/ servlet/ECCO> [accessed 2 June 2008].

5. *Treasures of Britain and Treasures of Ireland*, (London: Reader's Digest Association Ltd, 1990).

6. Worsley, *Classical Architecture*, p. 265. **NOTE THE USE OF AUTHOR AND SHORT TITLE FOR SECOND REFERENCE TO A SOURCE**

7. Peter Leach, 'James Paine's Design for the South Front of Kedleston Hall: Dating and Sources', *Architectural History*, 40 (1997),159-70.

8. Horace Walpole, cited in S. Lang, 'The Principles of the Gothic Revival in England', *Journal of the Society of Architectural Historians*, 25.4 (1966), 240-267. In *JSTOR*, <http://www.jstor.org/stable/988353> [accessed 3 June 2008]. **NOTE THIS IS A SECONDARY REFERENCE**

9. Alexandrina Buchanan, 'Interpretations of Medieval Architecture' In *Gothic Architecture and Its Meanings 1550-1830*, ed. by Michael Hall (Reading: Spire Books, 2002), pp. 27-52.

Note that in the footnote citations the authors' names appear with forename then surname.

Sample bibliography

The bibliography should include sources you have cited in footnotes and any sources you have read but not cited directly. In the bibliography the authors' names should appear in alphabetical order by surname.

The bibliography for the works cited in the sample text above would look like this:

Adam, Robert, *Ruins of the Palace of the Emperor Diocletian at Spalatro in Dalmatia*, London, (1764). In *Eighteenth Century Collections Online*, <http://galenet.galegroup.com/servlet/EC CO> [accessed 2 June 2008].

Buchanan, Alexandrina, 'Interpretations of Medieval Architecture' In *Gothic Architecture and Its Meanings 1550-1830*, ed. by Michael Hall (Reading: Spire Books, 2002), pp. 27-52.

Lang, S., 'The Principles of the Gothic Revival in England', *Journal of the Society of Architectural Historians*, 25.4 (1966), 240-267. In *JSTOR*, <http://www.jstor.org/stable/988353> [accessed 3 June 2008].

Leach, Peter, 'James Paine's Design for the South Front of Kedleston Hall: Dating and Sources', *Architectural History*, 40 (1997),159-70.

Nappo, Salvatore Ciro, *Pompeii: Its Discovery and Preservation*, (2003), <http://www.bbc.co.uk/history/ancient/romans/pompeii_rediscovery_01.shtml> [accessed 2 June 2008].

Palladio's Italian Villas, (2005), <http://www.boglewood.com/palladio/> [accessed 2 June 2008].

Treasures of Britain and Treasures of Ireland, (London: Reader's Digest Association Ltd, 1990).

Worsley, Giles, *Classical Architecture in Britain: The Heroic Age*. (London: Published for the Paul Mellon Centre for Studies in British Art by Yale University Press, 1995).

For further information on the MHRA referencing style, see the Association's website http://www.mhra.org.uk/.

F. Glossary

Abstract: A brief summary of an article or a book that also includes its reference information.

Address bar: Also known as location or URL bar, it indicates the current URL, web page address, path to a local file or other item to be located by the browser.

Bibliography: A list of **all** the sources that you consulted for your work arranged in alphabetical order by author's surname or, when there is no author, by title. For web pages where no author or title is apparent the url of the web page would be used.

Browser: A program with an interface for displaying HTML files, used to navigate the World Wide Web.

Citation: The in-text reference which gives brief details (e.g. author, date, page number) of the source that you are quoting from or referring to. This citation corresponds with the full details of the work (title, publisher etc.) given in your reference list or bibliography, so that the reader can identify and/or locate the work. End-text citations are more commonly known as references.

Common knowledge: Facts which are generally known.

Copyright: The legal protection given to authors which protects them against unauthorised copying of their work.

Direct quotation: The actual words used by an author, in exactly the same order as in their original work. See **Section B** for more details of how to set out all quotations in your text.

Ellipsis: The omission of words from speech or writing. A set of three dots ... shows where the original words have been omitted.

End-text citation: An entry in the reference list at the end of your work which contains the full (bibliographical) details of information for the in-text citation.

et al.: (From the Latin *et alii* meaning "and others") A term most commonly used (e.g. Harvard author-date system) for works having more than three authors. The citation gives the first surname/last name listed in the publication, followed by *et al*. As shown here, *et al*. should always be in italics.

Footnotes/Endnotes: Explanatory note and/or source citation either at the foot of the page or end of a chapter used in numeric referencing styles, eg MHRA.

HTML: The abbreviation for hypertext markup language – the language used for writing files on the Internet.

HTTP: The abbreviation for hypertext transfer (or transport) protocol. HTTP forms the set of rules for transferring files (text, images, sound etc.) on the Internet.

Hypertext: A system which allows extensive cross-referencing between related sections of text.

ibid.: (From the Latin *ibidem* meaning "in the same place") A term which refers to a previously cited work. It is not used in the Harvard system, where works appear only once in the alphabetical list of references.

Indirect quotation: A piece of text which you incorporate into your own text by making only minor changes to the wording. You must always cite and reference the quotation.

Internet: The global computer network which provides a variety of information and communication facilities, consisting of interconnected networks using standardised communication protocols.

In-text citation: Often known as simply the citation, this gives brief details (e.g. author, date, page number) of your source of information within your text.

op.cit.: (From the Latin *opere citato* meaning "in the work already cited"). A term not used in the Harvard system, where works appear only once in the alphabetical list of references.

Paraphrase: A restating of someone else's thoughts or ideas in your own words. You must always cite your source when paraphrasing. (See p.16 for more details and examples)

Parentheses: Another name for round brackets.

Peer-review: A process used in academic publishing to check that the accuracy and quality of a work intended for publication. The author's draft of a book or article is sent by an editor (usually anonymously) to experts in the subject, who suggest amendments or corrections. This process is seen as a guarantee of academic quality and is a major distinction between traditional forms of publishing such as books and journals, and information in web pages, which can be written by anyone even if they have no expertise in a subject.

Plagiarism: Taking and using another person's thoughts, writings or inventions as your own without acknowledging or citing the source of the ideas and expressions. In the case of copyrighted material, plagiarism is illegal.

Primary source: An original source, such as someone's manuscript, diary or journal, a survey or interview, letters, autobiographies, and observations.

Proper noun: The name of an individual person, place or organisation, having an initial capital letter.

Quotation: The words or sentences from another information source used within your text (see also Direct quotation and Indirect quotation above).

Reference: The full publication details of the work cited.

Reference list: A list of references at the end of your assignment which includes the full information for your citations so that the reader can easily identify and retrieve each work (journal articles, books, web pages etc.).

Secondary referencing: A piece of work that has been referred to in something you have read. See p.18 for more details and examples.

Secondary source: Material that is not the original manuscript, contemporary record or document associated with an event, but which critiques, comments on or builds upon primary sources. Examples of secondary sources are textbooks, journal articles, histories, criticisms, commentaries and encyclopaedias.

Short citations: Used in Numeric referencing systems, including MHRA and OSCOLA, instead of *op. cit.* When a work is cited for the first time, all bibliographic details are included in the footnotes/endnotes and in the bibliography reference. If a work is cited more than once in the text, the second and subsequent entries in the footnotes/endnotes use an abbreviated form or short citation, such as the author and title (as well as a specific page reference), so that the reader can find the full bibliographic details in the bibliography.

sic: (From the Latin meaning "so, thus") A term used after a quoted or copied word to show that the original word has been written exactly as it appears in the original text, and usually highlights an error or misspelling of the word.

Summary: Similar to a paraphrase, a summary provides a brief account of someone else's ideas or work; only the main points are covered, with the details being left out. (See p.17 for more details and examples).

Superscript number: A number used in numeric referencing styles (including MHRA and OSCOLA) to identify citations in the text, which is usually smaller than and set above the normal text, i.e.[1]

URL: The abbreviation for Uniform (or Universal) Resource Locator, the address of documents and other information sources on the Internet (e.g. http://...).

verbatim: An exact reproduction (word-for-word) of a sentence, phrase, quote or other sequence of text from one source into another such as your assignment.

Web page: A hypertext document accessible via the World Wide Web.

World Wide Web: The extensive information system on the Internet which provides facilities for documents to be connected to other documents by hypertext links.

G. Further reading

Plagiarism

Academy JISC Academic Integrity Service (2008) Available at: http://www.heacademy.ac.uk/ourwork/learn ing/collaboration/academic_integrity (Accessed: 4 July 2008).

Carroll, J. (2002) *Handbook for deterring plagiarism in higher education*. Oxford: Oxford Centre for Staff and Learning Development.

Higher Education and Research Opportunities in the United Kingdom (2005) *Plagiarism*. Available at: http://www.hero.ac.uk/uk/studying/guidanc e_and_support/studying_and_learning/pla giarism.cfm (Accessed: 4 July 2008).

JISC Internet Plagiarism Advisory Service (2008) *Why do students plagiarise?* Available at: http://www.jiscpas.ac.uk/documents/tipshe etsv3/tp02_WhyDoStudentsPlagiarise.pdf (Accessed: 4 July 2008)

Plagiarism: University of Leeds guide. (no date) Available at: http://www.lts.leeds.ac.uk/plagiarism/ (Accessed: 4 July 2008).

The challenge of original work. (no date) Available at http://www.princeton.edu/pr/pub/integrity/p ages/original.html (Accessed: 4 July 2008).

Stern, L. (2006) *What every student should know about avoiding plagiarism*. London: Longman.

Referencing

American Psychological Association (2008) *Electronic references*. Available at: http://www.apastyle.org/elecref.html (Accessed: 18 June 2008).

American Psychological Association (2001) *Publication Manual of the American Psychological Association*. Washington, D.C.: American Psychological Association.

The Bluebook: A uniform system of citation (2005) Harvard Law Review Association.

British Standards Institution. (1990). *BS 5605:1990. Recommendations for citing and referencing published material*. London: BSI.

The Chicago manual of style. 15th edn. (2003) Chicago: The University of Chicago Press.

Gibaldi, J. (2003) *MLA Handbook for Writers of Research Papers*. 6th edn. New York: Modern Language Association of America.

Great Britain. Ministry of Justice (2008) *How we cite legislation*. Available at: http://www.statutelaw.gov.uk/help/How_we _cite_legislation.htm (Accessed: 7 July 2008).

House of Commons Information Office (2008) *Factsheet G17: The Official Report*. Available at: http://www.parliament.uk/documents/uploa d/g17.pdf (Accessed: 2 July 2008).

Martin, P.W. (2007) *Introduction to basic legal citation*. Available at: http://www.law.cornell.edu/citation/ (Accessed: 6 July 2008).

Meredith, S. and Endicott, T. (2006) *OSCOLA: Oxford Standard for Citation of Legal Authorities*. Available at: http://denning.law.ox.ac.uk/published/oscola_2006.pdf (Accessed: 30 June 2008).

Modern Humanities Research Association (2008) *MHRA style guide: a handbook for authors, editors, and writers of theses*. 2nd edn. Available at: http://www.mhra.org.uk/Publications/Books/StyleGuide/index.html (Accessed: 6 June 2008).

Thomson, K. (2006) *Citing Scottish Parliament publications*. Available at: http://www.is.stir.ac.uk/research/citing/spcite.php (Accessed: 8 July 2008).

Further reading

Index

NB Hyphenated words are listed alphabetically by the word preceding the hyphen (eg e-mail before *Ebsco*)

Numbered entries below refer to pages

Index

Your notes